Pistol and Revolver Shooting

Pistol and Revolver Shooting

A. L. A. Himmelwright

LEONAUR

Pistol and Revolver Shooting
by A. L. A. Himmelwright

First published under the title
Pistol and Revolver Shooting

Leonaur is an imprint of Oakpast Ltd
Copyright in this form © 2013 Oakpast Ltd

ISBN: 978-1-78282-096-3 (hardcover)
ISBN: 978-1-78282-097-0 (softcover)

http://www.leonaur.com

Publisher's Notes

Contents

Preface

Interest in pistol and revolver shooting has increased very rapidly in recent years and particularly since smokeless powder has been introduced.

The revolver and the magazine pistol now constitute part of the regular equipment of army and navy officers and cavalry troops. Regulations governing practice shooting with these arms have been issued and adopted by both branches of the service and by the National Guard of the various States. In the National Rifle Association and in the various State rifle associations that have recently been organized, pistol and revolver shooting has an important place, and the matches provided are largely patronized. In the numerous civilian shooting clubs scattered throughout the country pistol and revolver shooting has become extremely popular, and in many cases the majority of the members practice more frequently with the smaller arms than with the rifle.

Practice with the pistol and revolver affords training in sighting, steady holding, and pulling the trigger, which are the essential features of rifle shooting also. On account of this relation, and the fact that skill with these arms can be instantly utilized in rifle shooting, the development of marksmanship with the pistol and revolver assumes national importance.

While numerous standard works have been written on the subject of rifle shooting, there is comparatively little information available on pistol and revolver shooting. The object of this volume is to supply practical information on this subject. The author has attempted to treat the subject in a clear and concise manner, keeping the size of the volume as small as practicable and so as to be conveniently carried in the pocket. Particular pains have been taken to give sound advice and elementary instruction to beginners.

The author extends his grateful acknowledgments to Baron Speck von Sternburg, Messrsr. J. B. Crabtree, John T. Humphrey, William E. Carlin, Chas. S. Axtell, Walter Winans, Walter G. Hudson, Ed. Taylor, J. E. Silliman, M. Hays, and the various arms and ammunition manufacturers referred to herein, for valuable assistance, suggestions, information and *data* in preparing this volume.

A. L. A. Himmelwright.

Stockholm, N. J.

CHAPTER 1

Introductory and Historical

Pistol shooting has been practiced ever since "grained" gunpowder came into general use. It is only recently, however, that it has developed into a popular pastime and has been recognized as a legitimate sport.[1]

The useful and practical qualities of the pistol and revolver have been developed almost wholly during the last half-century. Before this period the small arms designed to be fired with one hand were crude and inaccurate, and were intended to be used only at short range as weapons of defence. The single-barrelled muzzle-loading pistol has, nevertheless, been part of the army and navy officer's equipment since the sixteenth century. These pistols were of large calibre, smooth-bored, heavy, and unwieldy. The load was a spherical bullet and a large charge of powder. Enough accuracy was obtained to hit a man at 15 to 20 paces, which was deemed sufficient. The usefulness of these arms in action was limited to the firing of a single shot, and then using them as missiles or clubs.

The pistol in early days was considered a gentleman's arm—a luxury. It was the arm generally selected for duelling when that code was in vogue, the contestants standing 10 to 20 paces apart and firing at the word of command.

The development of the pistol has been contemporaneous and closely identified with that of the rifle. With the grooving or rifling of the barrel, the accuracy was greatly improved and the arm adapted to conical bullets. Although numerous attempts were made to devise a multishot arm with flint, wheel, and match locks, it was not until

---

1. The first pistols of which there is any authentic information were made about 1540 by one Caminelleo Vitelli at Pistoia, Italy, from which place the arm took its name.

the percussion cap was invented that a practicable arm of this character was produced. This was a "revolver" invented by Colonel Colt of Hartford, Conn., in 1835, and consisted of a single barrel with a revolving cylinder at the breech containing the charges, the mechanism being such that the cocking of the piece after each discharge revolved the cylinder sufficiently to bring a loaded chamber in line with the barrel.

The greatest advance in the development of firearms was the introduction of the system of breech-loading, employing ammunition in the form of cartridges. This principle rendered the operation of loading much simpler and quicker, and vastly improved the efficiency and general utility of the arms.[2]

The present popularity of pistol and revolver shooting is due, no doubt, to recent improvements in the arms and ammunition. The arms are now marvels of fine workmanship, easy to manipulate, durable, and extremely accurate. With the introduction of smokeless powders, the smoke, fouling, and noise have been reduced to a minimum. The effect of these improvements has been, not only to increase the efficiency of the arms, but also the pleasure of shooting them.

As a sport, pistol shooting has much to commend it. It is a healthful exercise, being practiced out-of-doors in the open air. There are no undesirable concomitants, such as gambling, coarseness, and rough and dangerous play. In order to excel, regular and temperate habits of life must be formed and maintained. It renders the senses more alert and trains them to act in unison and in harmony. But, above all, skill in shooting is a useful accomplishment.

Anyone possessing ordinary health and good sight may, by practice, become a good pistol shot. Persons who are richly endowed by nature with those physical qualities which specially fit them for expert shooting will, of course, master the art sooner than those less favoured; but it has been conclusively shown that excellence is more a question of training and practice than of natural gift. Some of the most brilliant shooting has been done by persons possessing a decidedly nervous temperament; but those of phlegmatic temperament will generally make more uniform and reliable marksmen.

2. For a detailed history of the evolution of the pistol and revolver, the reader is referred to *Text-book for Officers at Schools of Musketry*, Longman & Co., London; *Kriegstechnische Zeitschrift*, Heft I and II, 1901, Mittler & Sohn, Berlin; *The Modern American Pistol and Revolver*, Bradlee Whidden, Boston. Many interesting specimens of ancient and modern pistols and revolvers are owned and exhibited by the United States Cartridge Company of Lowell, Mass.

It is much more difficult to shoot well with the pistol or revolver than with the rifle. The latter, having a stock to rest against the shoulder and steady one end of the piece, has a decided advantage in quick aiming and in pulling the trigger. The former, without a stock and being held in one hand with the arm extended so as to be free from the body, is without any anchor or support whatever, and is free to move in all directions. Consequently the least jar, jerk in pulling the trigger, puff of wind, or unsteadiness of the hand greatly disturbs the aim. Intelligent practice will, however, overcome these difficulties and disadvantages to such a degree that an expert shot with a pistol or revolver under favorable conditions can equal a fair shot with a rifle at the target up to 200 yards. When the novice essays to shoot the pistol or revolver, the results are generally disappointing and discouraging; but rapid progress invariably rewards the efforts of those who persevere, and when once thoroughly interested in this style of shooting, there comes a fascination for it that frequently endures throughout a lifetime.

CHAPTER 2

Arms

The term "pistol" is frequently applied indiscriminately to the single-shot pistol and the revolver. A marked distinction between these arms has gradually been developed.

The pistol is now recognized as a single-shot arm, adapted for a light charge and designed to secure extreme accuracy. Its use is limited almost exclusively to target and exhibition shooting.

The modern revolver is an arm with a revolving cylinder holding five or six cartridges, which are at the instant command of the shooter before it is necessary to reload. It is designed for heavy charges, and is a practical and formidable weapon. Revolvers are made in great variety, and adapted for various purposes, such as military service, target shooting, pocket weapons, etc. The best grades of pistols and revolvers may be had at a reasonable price. The cheap grades with which the market is at all times flooded should be avoided. They are incapable of doing good work, and frequently are positively dangerous, on account of being made of inferior materials.

The magazine or automatic pistol is the latest type of hand firearm. It is a multishot pistol in which the mechanism is operated automatically by the recoil. Pulling the trigger is the only manual operation necessary to fire successive shots until the supply of cartridges in the magazine (usually six to ten) is exhausted. The first models were introduced about 1898. These had many defects and objections, such as failure to function regularly, danger in manipulation due to insufficient safety devices, poor balance, unsightly lines, etc. Nevertheless the advantages of this type of arm over the revolver for military purposes in effective range, rapidity of fire, accuracy, interchangeability, etc., were soon recognized and manufacturers were encouraged to improve and perfect them.

Practically all the mechanical defects referred to have been corrected, the balance and the lines improved, and safety devices introduced so that these arms are now well adapted for military use and are rapidly superseding the revolver as service weapons in the United States Army and Navy. A synopsis of the severe tests leading to the adoption of a magazine pistol by the War Department of the United States Government may be found in the Appendix.

Military Arms.—The revolver and the magazine pistol are used for military service. To fulfil the requirements these arms must be strong, very durable, and withstand a great amount of hard usage without becoming disabled. The effectiveness, or "stopping power," is of prime importance. The calibre should be large, the bullet should have a blunt point, and the powder charge should be sufficiently powerful to give a penetration of at least six inches in pine. There was a tendency some years ago to reduce the calibre of military revolvers. While this resulted in increased velocity and penetration, and reduced the weight of the ammunition, it did not improve the stopping power of the arms.

The ineffectiveness of the .38-calibre service revolver charge was frequently complained of by the officers and men serving in the Philippine Islands. This was due to the light powder charge and the conoidal shaped point of the bullet. To remedy this weakness .45-calibre revolvers were issued for the Philippine service, and a new .45-calibre cartridge designed to which magazine pistol manufacturers were invited to adapt an arm. Unfortunately this new cartridge, which is now the service ammunition, has also a conoidal pointed bullet, is not well proportioned, and consequently develops only a part of its stopping power possibilities.

The sights must in all cases be very substantial, and solidly fixed to the frame or barrel. The trigger pull varies from 4 to 8 pounds, the barrel from 4 to 7½ inches in length, and the weight from 2 to 2¾ pounds. Ammunition loaded with smokeless powder is now invariably used for military service.

The service revolvers still in use in the United States Army and Navy are the Smith & Wesson and Colt, both .38 calibre, and taking the same ammunition. They have passed the prescribed series of tests as established by the United States Government,[1] and as improved and perfected represent, without doubt, the highest development of the military revolver.

1. See Ordnance Reports, Department of War, Washington, D. C., for complete details of tests, etc.

These arms, shown in Figs. 1 and 2, have solid frames, and the actions are almost identical, the cylinder swinging out to the left, on a hinge, when released by a catch. The shells may then be extracted simultaneously by pushing back the extractor rod. The Smith & Wesson has an additional hinge-locking device in front of the cylinder. The Colt has an automatic safety lock between the hammer and the frame, permitting discharge only when the trigger is pulled. Apart from these features there is very little difference between these arms.

The Smith & Wesson .44-calibre Military Revolver is the latest model of the large calibre revolvers. Its action and general lines are the same as the .38-calibre military, but it is a larger, heavier, and more powerful weapon.

Other excellent military revolvers are the Colt New Service and the Smith& Wesson Russian model, usually in .45 calibre and .44 calibre, respectively. The ammunition for these arms was formerly loaded with black powder; but smokeless cartridges have been adapted to them, which give slightly increased velocity and the same accuracy. (See Fig. 4.)

The Smith & Wesson Russian model has a hinge "tip-up" action, with an automatic ejecting device. The action is operated by raising a catch in front of the hammer. It is easy to manipulate and, on account of the accessibility of the breech, the barrel can be readily inspected and cleaned. This arm is single action. (See Fig. 5.)

The action of the Colt New Service is similar to that of the .38-calibre revolver shown in Fig. 2, with a solid frame. It is double action.

The Colt Officer's Model is identical in every respect with the Army Special except that it is fitted with adjustable target sights and may be had with lengths of barrel up to 7½ inches.

The foregoing arms, with good ammunition, are capable of making groups of ten shots on a 3-inch circle at 50 yards.

The Colt single action army is the most popular belt or holster weapon among ranchmen, cowboys, prospectors, and others. It has a solid frame, simple mechanism, and is exceedingly durable and reliable. The arm is operated by opening a gate on the right-hand side, back of the cylinder. The cartridges are inserted in the cylinder through the gate, the cylinder being revolved by hand until the respective chambers come opposite the gate. In the same manner the shells are ejected by pushing the extractor rod back into each of the chambers. (See Fig. 6.)

FIG. 1.—SMITH & WESSON 38 CAL. MILITARY REVOLVER
Six shots; 6½ inch barrel; weight, 1 lb., 15 oz.

FIG. 2.—COLT ARMY SPECIAL REVOLVER
Six shots; 6 inch barrel; weight, 2 lbs. 3 oz., .38 cal.

FIG 3.—SMITH & WESSON .44 CAL. MILITARY REVOLVER.
Six shots; 6½ inch barrel; weight 2 lbs. 6½ oz.

FIG. 4.—COLT NEW SERVICE REVOLVER
Six shots; 5½ inch barrel; weight, 2 lbs., 8 oz.; .45 cal.

FIG. 5.—SMITH & WESSON RUSSIAN MODEL REVOLVER
Six shots; 6½ inch barrel; weight, 39¼ oz.; .44 cal.

FIG. 6.—COLT SINGLE ACTION REVOLVER
Six shots; 5½ inch barrel; weight, 2 lbs. 6 oz.; .45 cal.

The Smith & Wesson Schofield Model, .45 calibre, was formerly a United States service weapon. The ammunition for this arm, while less powerful than the .45 Colt, was admirably adapted for military service, and had much less recoil.

The Webley & Scott W. S. Model revolver is an English arm of much merit. The calibre is .455. It has a hinge "tip-up" action, with an automatic extractor very similar to the Smith & Wesson. (See Fig. 7.)

The service weapon adopted by the Joint War Office and Admiralty Committee for the British army and navy is the Webley & Scott "Mark IV," or "Service Model," revolver. This model is almost identical with the W. S. Model, except that the barrel is 4 inches long and the weight is 2 lbs. 3 oz. On account of the short barrel, the accuracy of this weapon does not equal that of the W. S. Model.

Another English arm is the "Webley-Fosbury" automatic revolver. The recoil revolving the cylinder and cocking the hammer, it can be fired as rapidly as the automatic pistols. It is chambered for the .455 service cartridge loaded with 5½ grains of cordite. This arm has been introduced since 1900. (See Fig. 8.)

Among the leading magazine or automatic pistols used for military service are the Colt, Luger, Webley & Scott, Savage, Mauser, Knoble, Bergmann, White-Merrill, Steyr, Mannlicher, Mors and Bayard. Most of these arms were tested by the United States government [2] previous to the adoption of the Colt as the service weapon of the U. S. Army and Navy. (See Fig. 9.) The Colt Automatic Pistol is now supplied with the automatic grip safety in all models. This prevents the discharge of the weapon unless properly held.

The Luger has been adopted as the service weapon by Germany, Switzerland, Portugal, Bulgaria, Holland, and Brazil. (See Fig. 10.)

The Webley-Scott (.455 calibre) was adopted as the service arm by the British navy in 1911, and the .32-calibre (weight 1 lb. 2 oz.) is now the adopted arm of the London City and Metropolitan police forces. (See Fig. 11.)

In most of these weapons, including the Colt, Webley & Scott, Luger, and Steyr pistols, the cartridges are inserted in magazines which feed them into the breech through the handle. In the Mauser pistol the cartridges are supplied through clips from the top and forced into a magazine located in front of the trigger. (See Fig. 12.)

The magazine pistols can be fired at the rate of about five shots per second. These arms equal the best military revolvers in accuracy.

2. See Appendix for digest of these tests.

FIG. 7.—WEBLEY & SCOTT "W. S." MODEL REVOLVER
Six shots; 7½ inch barrel; weight, 2 lbs., 7 oz.; .455 cal.

FIG. 8.—WEBLEY & FOSBURY AUTOMATIC REVOLVER.
Six shots; 6 inch barrel; weight, 2 lbs., 10 oz.; .455 cal.

FIG. 9.—COLT AUTOMATIC PISTOL.
Seven shots; 5 inch barrel; weight, 2 lbs. 7 oz.; .45 cal.

FIG. 10.—THE PARABELLUM OR "LUGER" AUTOMATIC
PISTOL
Eight shots; 4⁵/⁸ inch barrel; weight, 1 lb., 13.4 oz.; .30 cal.

FIG. 11.—WEBLEY & SCOTT AUTOMATIC PISTOL
Eight shots; 5 inch barrel; weight, 2 lbs., 7½ oz.; .455 cal.

FIG. 12.—MAUSER AUTOMATIC PISTOL
Ten shots; 5½ inch barrel; weight, 2 lbs., 7½ oz.; .30 cal.

Many persons believe that the magazine pistol will soon supersede the revolver for general use. While this may be the case eventually, it is not likely to occur within the next few years. The magazine pistol is more complicated, and consequently more difficult to learn to shoot with and care for, than the revolver. On account of the special problems to be solved in the mechanism, many of them balance poorly and the trigger pull is almost invariably long and creeping. The novice will also find it difficult to avoid flinching in shooting these arms, on account of the recoil mechanism, louder report, etc. The line of sight being considerably higher than the grip, if they are not held perfectly plumb, or in the same position at each shot, the shooting is liable to be irregular. The cost is more than that of a good revolver. Until these undesirable features can be remedied or eliminated, the revolver will probably remain a popular arm.

Target Arms.—For target purposes the greatest possible accuracy is desirable. To obtain this, many features essential in a military arm are sacrificed. Delicate adjustable sights are employed, the trigger pull is reduced, the length of the barrel is increased, the charge reduced, etc.

The most accurate arms available at the present time are the single-shot pistols manufactured by Smith & Wesson, Springfield, Mass., The J. Stevens Arms & Tool Co., Chicopee Falls, Mass.; Fred Adolph, Genoa, N.Y. These pistols are furnished in calibres from .22 rim-fire to .38 central-fire. The barrels are generally 10 inches in length and the trigger pull 2 pounds. In the latest approved form these pistols are of .22 calibre specially bored and chambered for the rim-fire, .22 calibre long rifle cartridge. This is a light, clean, pleasant shooting charge, and may be fired many times with very little fatigue. Pistol shooting with arms of this calibre is rapidly becoming a popular pastime for ladies as well as gentlemen.

The Smith & Wesson pistol has a tip-up action and an automatic extractor. It is made of the best materials and with the greatest care. The fitting and workmanship are superior to that of any other machine-made pistol. The action is similar to that of the Russian Model revolver. (See Fig. 13.)

The Stevens pistols were formerly furnished in three models and for many years they have enjoyed merited popularity for target shooting among the leading marksmen. This pistol is now supplied only in the No. 35 or "Offhand Target Model," which like the earlier models has a tip-up action and an automatic extractor. A small knob on the left side is pressed to release the barrel and operate the action. (See Fig. 14.)

The Remington pistol has an exceedingly strong action, and is the only machine-made pistol with an action adapted for regulation .44, .45, and .50 calibre cartridges. It has a large handle and a heavy barrel. The action is operated when the hammer is at full-cock by throwing back the breech-block with the thumb, simultaneously ejecting the empty shell. Unfortunately the manufacture of these weapons has recently been discontinued. (See Fig. 15.)

The Adolph-Weber pistol designed by M. Casimir Weber, of Zurich, Switzerland, is a high grade hand-made arm that can be supplied by Mr. Fred Adolph in accordance with any specifications that the marksman may desire. Fig. 16 illustrates it conforming to the rules and regulations of the U. S. Revolver Association. It has a strong, durable, tip-up action resembling in principle that of the Stevens, and when closed the barrel is securely locked in position by a cross bolt, actuated by a button on the left side. (See Fig. 16.)

The Adolph-Martini is a weapon *de luxe* that has been produced in the same manner as the Adolph-Weber, in which the action of the Martini rifle has been employed. It has double set triggers and is highly ornate.

The Adolph "H.V." is a .22 calibre pistol adapted for a special high velocity cartridge developing a muzzle velocity of 2,000 ft. per second and an energy of 623 foot-pounds.

With good ammunition all these pistols are capable of placing ten shots within a 2-inch circle at 50 yards.

A very accurate pistol for gallery and short-range shooting is made by M. Gastinne-Renette of Paris and used in his gallery in that city. These are muzzle-loading and are very tedious and inconvenient to manipulate. For this reason they have not become popular. A few of these arms have been made up as breech-loaders, with a tip-up action similar to the Stevens, but operated by a side lever under the hammer and chambered for the .44 Russian cartridge. In this form with gallery charges the pistol has given very good results. (See Fig. 17.)

The latest addition to the target arms is the Colt .22 cal. Automatic Pistol. It has a longer barrel than any other automatic pistol and is fitted with adjustable sights. It has good balance and the long distance between the sights makes excellent work at the target possible. (See Fig. 17a.)

The revolver is not quite as accurate as the pistol, on account of

FIG. 13.—SMITH & WESSON PISTOL
Ten-inch barrel; weight, 1 lb., 8¾ oz., .22 cal.

FIG. 14—STEVENS PISTOL, GOULD MODEL
Ten-inch barrel; weight, 1 lb., 10 oz.; .22 cal.

FIG. 15.—REMINGTON PISTOL
Ten-inch barrel, weight, 2 lbs., 8 oz.; .44 cal.

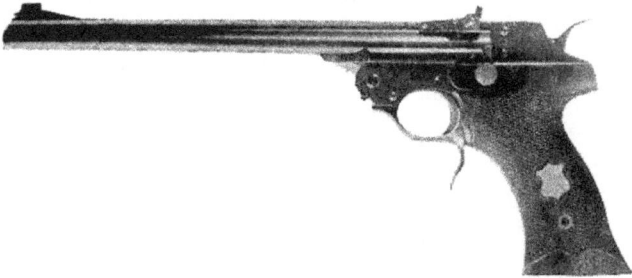

FIG. 16—ADOLPH WEBER PISTOL
Ten-inch barrel; weight, 2 lbs. 2 oz.; .22 cal.

FIG. 17—GASTINNE-RENETTE PISTOL
$10^{3/16}$ inch barrel; weight, 2 lbs. 6 oz.; .44 cal.

FIG. 17A—COLT AUTOMATIC TARGET PISTOL
Ten shots; 6½ inch barrel; weight, 28 oz.; .22 cal.

the necessity of having the cylinder detached from the barrel. If the pin on which the cylinder revolves is not at right angles with the end of the cylinder, there will be more space between the cylinder and the breech end of the barrel in some positions of the cylinder than in others. The result will be varying amounts of gas escaping from the different chambers of the cylinder, and consequently irregular shooting. The accuracy of the revolver depends largely, too, upon the degree of perfection in which all the chambers of the cylinder align with the bore of the barrel at the instant of discharge. When the chambers do not align perfectly, the bullet enters the barrel eccentrically and a portion of it is shaved off. This is fatal to accuracy, especially when smokeless powder is used. Imperfect alignment of chamber and barrel is also a frequent cause of the "leading" of the barrel. Some very ingenious mechanical expedients are used in the best revolvers to reduce to a minimum the wear of those parts which operate and hold the cylinder in position.

The revolvers generally used for target shooting are the military arms already described, with longer barrels, chambered for special cartridges, fitted with target sights, special handles, and other modifications to suit the whims and tastes of individuals.

Some of these modifications are distinctly advantageous. One of the most recent fads is to skeletonise the hammer by boring away as much metal as possible and to increase the tension of the main spring. The combined effect is almost instant response to the trigger pull.

The best and most experienced shots are careful to keep the modifications of all their arms within the rules and regulations of the various national organisations,[3] in order that they may be used in the annual competitions and other important events. These organizations control the pistol and revolver shooting, and conduct annual competitions. "Freak" arms which do not comply with the rules are not allowed in the competitions, are seldom practical, and have little or no value other than for experimental purposes. Target arms are generally used for trick and exhibition shooting.[4]

---

3. The United States Revolver Association, The National Rifle Association of Great Britain, and the United Shooting Societies of France. For programmes and details, address the secretaries of the respective organizations.
4. For descriptions and illustrations of this style of shooting, see *The Art of Revolver Shooting*, by Walter Winans (also published by Leonaur). This elaborate work contains also much detailed information, valuable suggestions, and many interesting personal experiences in relation to revolver shooting.

Pocket Arms.—The most extensive use of the revolver as a pocket weapon is for police service. Special arms are manufactured to meet the requirements. These weapons are generally similar to the military revolvers, but smaller in size and adapted for lighter charges. All projections, such as sights, hammer, etc., must be eliminated or minimized so as not to catch in drawing the arm from the pocket or holster. The barrels are usually from 3 to 5 inches in length, the trigger pull 4 pounds and the calibre .22 to .38. The larger calibres are much preferable for the general purposes of an arm of this character. The difference in weight is slight, while the power and effectiveness of the large calibres is important and a great advantage.

The pocket arms shown in Figs. 18 and 19 are practically reduced sizes of the military arms shown in Figs. 1 and 2. They have solid frames and actions identical with those of the military arms. The Smith & Wesson is made only in .32 calibre but the Colt may be had in .32 or .38. Both are double action.

The Colt Police Special is similar in model to Fig. 18 but is slightly larger and heavier and can be had chambered for the powerful .38 calibre Special, or the .32 calibre Winchester cartridges.

The Smith & Wesson Double Action, Perfected, is an improved model of this popular pocket weapon, having a double locking action. (See Fig. 20.)

One of the most popular pocket revolvers is the Smith & Wesson Safety Hammerless. This arm has a safety latch in the back of the handle, so designed that unless the piece is properly held it is impossible to operate it. It has many valuable and desirable features to commend it as a practical pocket weapon and for home protection. The standard length of barrel is 4 inches. This arm is also furnished in .32 calibre. (See Fig. 21.)

With 4-inch barrels, the foregoing pocket weapons are capable of shooting regularly within a 2-inch circle at 20 yards.

A heavier and correspondingly more powerful pocket revolver is the Colt "Double Action" revolver. This arm is chambered for the Colt .41 calibre short and long cartridges. It has a solid frame, and is operated exactly like the Colt Single Action Army Model (Fig 6). It is compact, strong, durable, and accurate.

For many years there was no high grade .22 calibre revolver on the market. Within the last few years two excellent arms in this calibre have been produced. The Smith & Wesson is supplied chambered only for the S. & W. long cartridges, but in two lengths of barrels; 3 inches

FIG. 18—COLT POLICE POSITIVE REVOLVER
Six shots; 4 inch barrel; weight, 1 lb., 4 oz.; .32 cal.

FIG. 19—SMITH & WESSON HAND EJECTOR REVOLVER
Six shots; 4½ inch barrel; weight, 18½ oz.; .32 cal.

FIG. 20.—SMITH & WESSON DOUBLE ACTION PERFECTED
REVOLVER
Five shots; 4 inch barrel; weight, 17¼ oz.; .38 cal.

with fixed sights and 6 inches with target sights. The Colt is furnished only in one length of barrel, 6 inches, but chambered for any of the rim-fire cartridges, and the .32 calibre short and long Colt, central-fire cartridges. These arms with 6-inch barrels are extremely accurate, pleasant to shoot on account of the light recoil and the ammunition is inexpensive. They are well adapted for target shooting for ladies and excellent for small game shooting. (See Figs. 22 and 23.)

A very handy little arm to carry in the pocket on hunting and fishing trips is the Stevens Diamond Model single-shot pistol. It is light in weight, very accurate, and low in cost. (See Fig. 24.)

All these .22 calibre arms can be depended on to kill grouse, ducks, rabbits, and other small game. The hollow-pointed bullet ammunition should be used, or the regular cartridge, with the front of the bullet cut off square, so as to leave a flat point. This will increase the killing effect of the bullet considerably.

Magazine pistols of smaller size than the military arms have in recent years become popular as pocket weapons. Such types as have safety devices to prevent discharge when the arm is not properly held for firing, are well adapted for this purpose.

The Colt Pocket Models are made in .38 calibre and .32 calibre as shown in Fig. 25, and in .25 calibre as illustrated in Fig. 26. This model is supplied with an additional safety which prevents accidental discharge in the event a cartridge is left in the barrel when the magazine is withdrawn.

The Savage Pocket Model is made in .38 and .32 calibre using the same cartridge as the Colt. It has an automatic indicator showing when the arm is loaded. A recent improvement in this arm is a spur cocking lever which permits cocking with the thumb of the hand holding the weapon. (See Fig. 27.)

The Smith & Wesson automatic is furnished only in .35 calibre. It has a wood stock backed by steel plates. The automatic safety in this arm is located in front of the trigger guard and is operated by the second finger. (See Fig. 28.)

As in the case of pocket revolvers, the larger calibres of the pocket automatic pistols will be found to have better stopping power and as practical weapons for use in case of emergency are to be preferred to the smaller calibres.

Persons who have very limited use for a weapon as for home protection and occasional pocket use, especially when they do not expect to practice shooting with it regularly will find a suitable revolver

FIG. 21.—SMITH & WESSON SAFETY HAMMERLESS
REVOLVER
Five shots; 4 inch barrel; weight, 1 lb., 1¼ oz.; .38 cal.

FIG. 22.—SMITH & WESSON POCKET REVOLVER
Seven shots; 3½ inch barrel; weight, 10 oz.; .22 cal.

FIG. 23—COLT POLICE POSITIVE TARGET REVOLVER
Seven shots; 6 inch barrel; weight, 1 lb., 6 oz.; .22 and .32 cal.

FIG. 24.—STEVENS DIAMOND MODEL PISTOL
Six inch barrel; weight, 8¾ oz.; .22 cal.

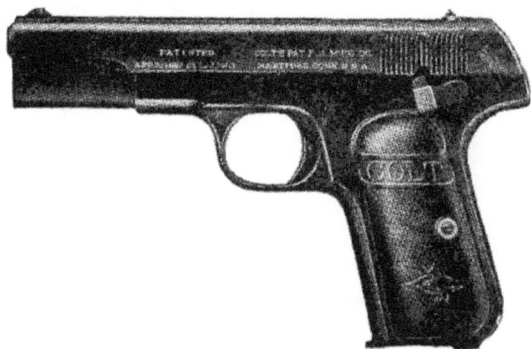

FIG. 25.—COLT AUTOMATIC POCKET PISTOL
Eight shots; 3¾ inch barrel; weight, 1 lb., 7 oz.; .32 and .38 cal.

much more serviceable, safer, and generally more satisfactory than a magazine pistol. The latter on account of its more complicated and concealed mechanism is liable to be left in an unserviceable condition for safety in the home (unloaded, magazines misplaced, etc.) and when needed, unfamiliarity with its manipulation not only causes delay in getting it in action but also is a fruitful source of accident. For the purpose referred to in this paragraph a .38 calibre Smith & Wesson Safety Hammerless, a .38 or .32 calibre Colt Police Positive, or a .32 calibre Smith & Wesson Hand Ejector with a 4-inch barrel and a 4-pound trigger pull in each case is recommended. Owners of such weapons for home or personal protection should practice with them occasionally, firing at least 20 or 25 shots. A good range for such practice is 20 to 30 feet. After using the arm it should in all cases be carefully cleaned and oiled as described under "Cleaning and Care of Arms."

CHAPTER 3

Ammunition

The degree of perfection that has been attained in the manufacture of ammunition is remarkable. Generally speaking, the smaller the charge the more difficult it is to make it accurate. Notwithstanding this, we have in the .22 calibre ammunition a tiny cartridge the accuracy of which falls little short of marvellous.

Until 1907 black powder ammunition was used almost exclusively for pistol and revolver shooting. In central-fire ammunition smokeless powders are now invariably used, especially in military shooting, where the regulation full charge is required. In the .22 calibre pistols, the fouling of the black powder is not a very serious matter, and it is not uncommon to shoot fifty or a hundred rounds without the necessity of cleaning. In the larger calibres, however, the fouling is frequently so excessive that it affects the accuracy after the fifth shot. The incessant cleaning that is necessary in order to get good results with black powder ammunition was a great drawback, and detracted much from the pleasure of revolver shooting. Fortunately this objection is now entirely eliminated by the use of smokeless powders.

Nearly all the cartridges referred to in this chapter were originally designed for black powder. The various manufacturers now supply them loaded with smokeless powder at a very slight advance in price. The cartridges are loaded so as to give approximately the same velocity as the former black powder charges but the new charges are rarely the exact equivalent of the old ones.

The accuracy and uniformity with the smokeless powder was not at first equal to that of the black, but with a better knowledge of the action and behaviour of the smokeless powders, these difficulties have been overcome and the smokeless ammunition now gives not only superior accuracy and reliability, but also causes much less fouling and

31

FIG 26 COLT AUTOMATIC POCKET PISTOL
Seven shots; 2 inch barrel; weight, 13 oz.: 25 cal.

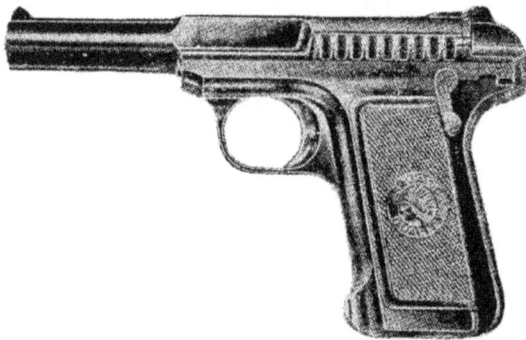

FIG. 27—SAVAGE AUTOMATIC POCKET PISTOL
Ten shots; 4¼ inch barrel; weight, 1 lb. 5 oz.; .32 and .38 cal.

FIG. 28.—SMITH & WESSON AUTOMATIC POCKET PISTOL
Eight shots; 3½ inch barrel; weight, 1 lb., 7¾ oz.; .35 cal.

smoke and has a lighter report. In "gallery" ammunition light conical bullets have entirely superseded spherical bullets and smokeless powder is almost invariably used.

To obtain the best results, the proportions of any charge must be adapted to the calibre, length of barrel, and weight of the arm in which it is to be used. These proportions are generally determined by experiment.

The accuracy of the cartridge depends largely upon the uniformity exercised in the operations of loading, the fit of the bullet, its shape, and the reliability and uniformity of the powder. The primer must be of uniform strength also, especially in reduced charges. In ammunition for military service the shells are crimped on the bullets to hold them in place. This does not increase the accuracy in black powder ammunition, but it is necessary and advantageous in all smokeless ammunition including gallery charges, in order to confine the powder and produce uniform results.

The following is a digest of the principal pistol and revolver cartridges in use at the present time.

Rim-fire Cartridges.—These are primed with a fulminate of mercury mixture around the outer edge of the rim, or base of the shell, and are generally loaded with Lesmok, semi-smokeless, or black powder.

FIGURE 29.

The smallest and lightest charged ammunition in general use is the .22 calibre. In this calibre the "C. B." or Conical Ball Cap loaded with black powder is the smallest practicable cartridge. The charge is 1½ grains of powder and a lubricated conical bullet weighing 29 grains.

FIGURE 30.

An excellent cartridge in this calibre is the .22 short, (Fig. 30). This cartridge fouls very little and is almost equal in accuracy to the .22 "long rifle" up to 50 yards. On account of its lighter report it is preferred by many for gallery shooting.

FIGURE 31.

The .22 calibre "long rifle" cartridge is more extensively used for pistol shooting than any other. It is the most accurate of the .22-calibre cartridges, being well proportioned, the bullet well lubricated, and the shell uncrimped. In addition to this, the ammunition is inexpensive and has very clean shooting qualities. It is, therefore, particularly well adapted for pistol shooting. This cartridge, fired from a 10-inch barrel, will shoot regularly inside of a 2-inch circle, at 50 yards, and inside a 5-inch circle at 100 yards.

The .22-calibre Long Rifle "Armoury" and the .22-calibre Smith & Wesson Long are special makes of the long rifle cartridge that are furnished with a crimped shell, preventing the bullet from becoming dislodged and thus adapting this popular cartridge for use in revolvers of this calibre.

In all of the foregoing cartridges only the surface of the bullet outside the shell is lubricated. Exposed in this way, the lubricant is easily rubbed off, or melted if allowed to stand in the sunlight on a warm day. Great care should be taken to prevent this, as, without lubrication, the bullets will lead the barrel and cause inaccurate shooting.

FIGURE 32.

The .22-calibre Winchester is a cartridge with inside lubrication. It is more powerful than the .22 long rifle, and gives good results in the pistol. The bullet has a flat point, making it suitable for game shooting, and the lubrication being within the shell, these cartridges may be carried loose in the pocket.

All of the .22 calibre cartridges can be had with hollow-pointed bullets, which are to be preferred for game shooting. They are also furnished loaded with smokeless powder. When this powder was first used in .22-calibre ammunition the results were far from satisfactory, but as now manufactured the smokeless ammunition approximates very closely in uniformity and accuracy to that loaded with black powder.

There still remains, however, considerable difficulty with the rim-fire smokeless cartridges on account of their liability to rust the inside of the barrel.[1] The novice is therefore cautioned not to use this ammunition until the difficulty of rusting is overcome.

The .25-cal. Stevens is a much more powerful cartridge than any of the preceding, and gives excellent results in the pistol. It is selected by those who wish a more powerful rim-fire cartridge than is furnished in .22 calibre.

FIGURE 33.

Rim-fire cartridges in larger calibre than .25 are used for der-ringers (large-bore, single-shot pocket pistols now seldom used) and inferior grades of revolvers. These cartridges sometimes lack uniformity in calibre when made by different manufacturers, are frequently defective, and discharge occasionally in closing the action of the arm in which they are loaded. They consequently lack the safety, reliability, and accuracy of the corresponding calibres in central-fire ammunition. Rim-fire cartridges cannot be reloaded.

Central-fire Cartridges.—This type of cartridge has a brass or copper

---

1. The difficulty is probably caused by the priming composition used at the present time in smokeless rim-fire ammunition. These compositions vary with different manufacturers, but most of them contain fulminate of mercury, chlorate of potash, powdered glass, etc. The trouble is probably caused principally by the chlorate of potash and perhaps by the fulminate of mercury. At any rate, a corrosive residue is left which attacks the barrel and causes it to rust. A priming composition free from deleterious substances, and which will not leave a corrosive residue, is urgently needed for both rim-fire and centre-fire ammunition.

primer fitted with a skeleton anvil of brass and charged with a small quantity of priming composition containing a sensitive explosive for igniting the powder charge. The primer fits water-tight in a socket in the centre of the base of the shell. After being discharged, the primer can be renewed and the shell reloaded. In all the central-fire cartridges the lubrication of the bullet is inside of the shell, rendering the ammunition much more serviceable and less liable to be damaged.

Mantled bullets designated as "metal pointed" and "full metal patched" can be supplied by the ammunition manufacturers for all the central-fire cartridges at a cost of one dollar per thousand more than the regular lead bullets. The mantled bullets do not deform as readily in handling, shipping, etc., and give slightly increased penetration in soft woods, animal tissue, etc., as compared with the plain lead bullet with the same powder charge.

FIGURE 34.   FIGURE 35.

The .32-calibre S. & W. cartridge is adapted to the Smith & Wesson, Colt, or other pocket revolvers. Occasionally single-shot pistols are chambered for this cartridge. It is fairly accurate at ranges up to 50 yds. A gallery charge is furnished in this shell consisting of 4 grains of black powder and a spherical or "round" bullet weighing 47 grains.

The .32-cal. S. & W. Long is more accurate and powerful than the preceding cartridge. It gives excellent results in both the pistol and revolver. The gallery charge is the same as that of the .32 S. & W.

The .32-calibre Colt New Police is also an accurate cartridge, and was designed specially for the Colt New Police revolver. The flat point adds to its effectiveness. A good gallery charge in this shell consists of a powder charge of 1½ grains of Bullseye and the regular bullet.

FIGURE 36.

The .32-44 S. & W. and the .38-44 S. & W. were special black powder cartridges designed for the S. & W. Russian Model revolver bored for these calibres. The shells were uncrimped and the bullets seated inside of the shells flush with the mouth. A large variety of special bullets of varying weights were designed for these cartridges and much experimentation was done with them. The .38-44 Calibre was originally designed for and largely used by Chevalier Ira A. Paine, the noted pistol shot in his exhibitions.

While these cartridges proved very accurate and were popular when black powder was in general use they are entirely unsuited for smokeless powders and consequently are now seldom used.

The .38 S. & W. is adapted to the Smith & Wesson, Colt, and other pocket revolvers. It is much more powerful than the .32 S. & W., and is consequently more practical and better adapted for a pocket revolver charge. When shot from a 4-inch barrel, groups of ten shots can be made in a 2-inch circle at 20 yards and in a 6-inch circle at 50 yards.

A good gallery or reduced load in this shell is Ideal Bullet No. 358242, 36072, or 360302 with 2 grains of Bullseye powder.

FIGURE 37.

FIGURE 38.

The .38 Colt New Police is almost identical with the .38 S. & W., the only difference being a slightly heavier bullet with a flat point.

FIGURE 39.

The .38 Long Colt is adapted to the Colt and S. & W. Military revolvers. It was the regulation charge of the service weapon of the U.S. Army until 1911. Under service conditions the cartridge was found to have insufficient power, was inaccurate and on account of the deterioration of the powder with which some of the ammunition was loaded it proved most unsatisfactory, especially in the Philippine war.

FIGURE 40.

The .38 Smith & Wesson Special cartridge is more powerful than the .38 Long Colt and is exceedingly accurate. From a 6-inch barrel six shots may be placed within a 5-inch circle at 100 yards. Numerous gallery and mid-range charges with special bullets have been designed for this cartridge. It is now the most popular of all the revolver cartridges for target practice. Some of the special bullets are illustrated herewith, the numbers being those used in the "Ideal Handbook":

358242	360345	36072

125 GR.	115 GR.	110 GR.

360302	360271	360363

112 GR.	150 GR.	70 GR.

FIGURE 41.

A powder charge of 2¼ to 2½ grains of Bullseye will give good results with any of these bullets. Bullets No. 360345, 360302 and 360271

38

cut full-size bullet holes in the targets.

The following are some of the special charges supplied by the manufacturers in this shell:

Name	Manu-facturer	Weight in Grains	Powder Charge	Wt. in grains Bullets	Type Bullet
Gallery	U. M. C. Co.	5.2	Black	70	Spherical
Target	U. M. C. Co.	2.6	Bullseye	130	R. N.
Colt Special	U. M. C. Co.	3.4	Bullseye	160	F. N.
Sharp Shoulder	U. M. C. Co.	2.1	Bullseye	122	F. Head
Mid Range	Winchester	2.0	Bullseye	104	R. N.
Gallery	Winchester	8 5	C. P. W.	70	R N.

The .44-calibre Smith & Wesson Russian[2] was the most popular revolver cartridge for target shooting before smokeless powder was introduced. Since smokeless charges have been adapted to it many expert shots prefer this cartridge in the gallery contests as the large bullet hole is a decided advantage over the smaller calibres at ranges of 20 yards and under.

Nearly all the great records in revolver shooting in the past have been made with this cartridge and many important matches have been won with it. A great deal of experimental work has also been done with it, and many reduced charges have been evolved. The Ideal Manufacturing Company can furnish moulds for bullets of the shapes and weights shown in Fig. 43.

FIGURE 42

---

2. So named after its adoption as the service ammunition of the Russian cavalry.

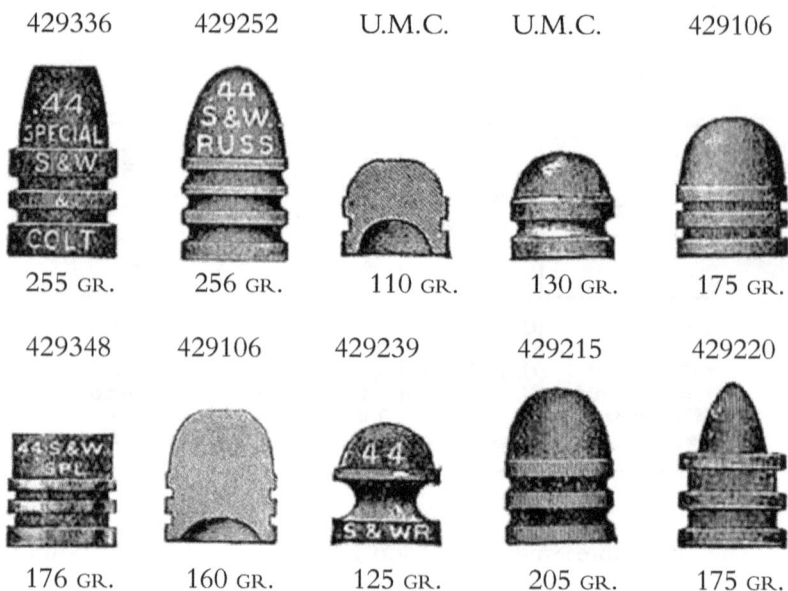

429336	429252	U.M.C.	U.M.C.	429106
255 GR.	256 GR.	110 GR.	130 GR.	175 GR.
429348	429106	429239	429215	429220
176 GR.	160 GR.	125 GR.	205 GR.	175 GR.

FIGURE 43.

Bullets No. 429336, 429348, and 429220 cut clean, full-size holes in the target. The weight of the powder charge and bullets in grains and the accuracy of the various loads fired from 6½-inch barrel are about as follows:

Bullseye Powder	Bullet	Diameter of Circle Enclosing Group of 10 Shots				
		20 yds.	30 yds.	50 yds.	100 yds.	200 yd.
4.1	256	1 in.	1½ in.	1¼ in.	6 in.	15 in.
2.3	110	1 in.	2 in.			
2.7	130	1¼ in.	2½ in.			
3.0	160		2 in.	3 in.		
2.8	176	1½ in.				
3.0	175		2½ in.			
2.7	125	1¼ in.	2¼ in.			
3.2	205		2 in.	3 in.	7 in.	
2.6	175	1¼ in.		3¼ in.		

These various loads adapt this shell to almost any conceivable requirement in revolver shooting.

FIGURE 44.

The .44 S. & W. Special is the latest and most powerful of the .44-calibre cartridges. It equals the .44 S. & W. Russian in accuracy and is the best proportioned of the heavy revolver cartridges. The reduced and gallery loads of the .44 S. & W. Russian will give equally good results in this shell.

FIGURE 45.

The .45 Colt Army is the most powerful of all the revolver cartridges. It was formerly the United States army service ammunition. The charge was so heavy, and the recoil so excessive that it was almost impossible to shoot it without flinching. The smokeless powder charge of 5 grains of Bullseye makes it much more practical and very similar to the .44 S. & W. Special cartridge. Both of these are exceedingly powerful and accurate and suitable for military service.

FIGURE 46.

FIGURE 47.

The calibre of the service ammunition for the revolver of the British army is .455. This is a very accurate cartridge, but not as powerful as the corresponding military cartridges used in this country. A special cylindrical bullet with a deep convex hollow point is furnished[Pg 52] in the same shell and is known as the "man stopper."

41

This form of bullet is used in the English .450 and .38 calibre cartridges also.

The .450 Welby is another English cartridge that is accurate, and pleasant to shoot. It is used largely at Bisley in the annual revolver competitions of the National Rifle Association of Great Britain.

In order to avoid excessive fouling with black powders a self-lubricating bullet has been invented and introduced by Smith & Wesson, which can be furnished in all calibres above .32. The bullet has a hollow core open in the rear. Lubricant is filled into the core, after which it is closed with a lead plunger. Four small ducts communicate from the forward end of the core to the exterior of the bullet just ahead of its bearing on the barrel. At the moment of discharge the plunger is driven forward, forcing the lubricant through the ducts into the barrel ahead of the bullet.

This bullet has given excellent results and will be found decidedly advantageous when black powder is used. With it a hundred or more shots may be fired with black powder without causing sufficient fouling to impair the accuracy.

Revolvers are sometimes chambered for the .44-40-200, the .38-40-180, and the .32-20-115 rifle cartridges. These charges in black powder load are not as accurate as the corresponding revolver cartridges in these calibres, but can be relied on to shoot inside a 5-inch circle at 50 yards. These cartridges are desirable for revolvers only when it is an advantage to use the same ammunition in the rifle and revolver, or in certain localities where only a few varieties of ammunition are to be had. The large powder charge makes the recoil of the first two cartridges named rather unpleasant. The .32-20-115 is the most accurate of these cartridges, and gives the best results in the pistol or revolver.

All these cartridges having flat-pointed bullets are well adapted for game shooting. None of these rifle cartridges loaded with smokeless powder will give good results in revolvers because the brand of powder generally used in rifle ammunition requires a long barrel to consume the charge. Fired from a short barrel only part of the charge will be consumed and the rest will be expelled unburned, thus reducing the velocity and power of the charge and sometimes increasing the recoil. It is of course entirely practicable to adapt a charge of bullseye or similar smokeless powder to these shells which would make them much more satisfactory.

Another disadvantage of using the rifle cartridge in revolvers is the possibility of inexperienced persons using the new high velocity rifle ammunition, which would prove not only most unsatisfactory but extremely dangerous in revolvers. There are no reduced or gallery loads supplied in these shells.

FIGURE 48.

FIGURE 49.

FIGURE 50.

FIGURE 51.

FIGURE 52.

FIGURE 53.

Automatic Pistol Cartridges.—With the introduction of the magazine pistol special smokeless cartridges have been devised that are rimless and have a crease around the base of the shell by which they may be held and manipulated by the mechanism. These cartridges are exceedingly clean-shooting. Several hundred rounds may be fired without causing more fouling than is apparent after the first few shots. This ammunition is furnished loaded with "full-mantled" and "soft-nosed" bullets; the latter, having the lead exposed at the point will mushroom on striking animal tissue and are sometimes referred to as "dum dum" bullets and are intended for hunting purposes.

FIGURE 54.

FIGURE 55.

FIGURE 57.   FIGURE 56.

The mantled or metal cased bullet has undoubted advantages in rifle ammunition, in which low trajectory and extreme long range are *desiderata* that can be obtained only by high velocities. In ammunition for magazine pistols and revolvers, however, the prime object is to deliver the most effective blow possible at comparatively short range.

The velocities attainable in large calibres within the permissible weight of an automatic pistol are comparatively low. The deformation of any bullet on striking animal tissue is in direct proportion to its velocity. It is, therefore, extremely doubtful that a metal cased bullet will ever prove as effective and satisfactory in "stopping power" and for military service, either in the automatic pistol or the revolver, as the large calibre lead bullet.

The .25 cal. is the smallest of the American made automatic pistol ammunition and is adapted for the Colt and other magazine pistols. It is an accurate cartridge but the short length of barrel of the Colt weapon makes it impossible to do accurate work with it.

Figures 49 and 50 are the well known Luger and Mauser cartridges adapted to the pistols of that name. They are powerful charges, accurate and clean shooting. These were among the first cartridges developed for automatic pistols and are still extensively used.

The .32 Automatic Colt is adapted to Colt and other magazine pistols of this calibre. It is an accurate, pleasant shooting cartridge with very little recoil and excellent work can be done with it at the target.

The .35 S. & W. Automatic is adapted to the Smith & Wesson magazine pistol. It is a very accurate cartridge, has no unpleasant recoil and like the preceding is well adapted for target shooting.

Figure 53 is the .380 Automatic Colt cartridge designed to meet the demand for a light charge in this calibre. It is adapted to the Colt and other magazine pistols.

The .38 Automatic Colt is the best proportioned and most powerful of all automatic pistol cartridges. It has a slightly flattened point and is extremely accurate. When fired from regulation arms this am-

44

munition is capable of placing ten shots inside a 3-inch circle at 50 yards and inside a 7-inch circle at 100 yards.

This was the ammunition of the first Colt automatic pistol introduced in the United States.

Figures 55 and 56 are two cartridges adapted to the .45 Automatic Colt pistol. Figure 56 is the new service charge of the U. S. Army. They are exactly alike except that the service charge has a 230 gr. bullet (30 gr. heavier than the other). The service charge when fired from the regulation service arm is capable of placing 10 shots in a 3½-inch circle at 50 yards and an 8-inch circle at 100 yards.

A flat or blunt pointed bullet of about 185 gr. and a ten *per cent. heavier powder charge would improve the effectiveness and stopping* power of this cartridge wonderfully without materially affecting the recoil or the accuracy.

Figure 57 is the service charge of the regulation magazine pistol (Webley& Scott) of the British Army. It is an accurate cartridge but it lacks sufficient power to fulfil the exacting requirements of present-day military service.

Light or gallery charges in magazine pistol shells are impracticable on account of not having sufficient recoil to operate the automatic mechanism. Slightly reduced loads with lead bullets may be used in some of the arms but seldom with satisfactory results. Reduced loads can be used in most of the weapons if the mechanisms are hand operated for each shot.

The following ballistical table gives the charges, muzzle velocities, etc., of the principal factory-loaded, smokeless pistol and revolver cartridges. The factories aim to keep the muzzle velocities uniform for each cartridge. To produce this result with the various brands of smokeless powder, all of which differ more or less in strength, the weight of the powder charge necessarily varies for the different brands of powder. Even when purchased in large quantities, different blends and packages of the same brand of powder occasionally vary somewhat in strength. For these reasons it is impossible to designate the exact weight or volume of any brand of powder which will in all cases produce the muzzle velocities in the table, and the charges given must therefore be considered as approximate only.

BALLISTICAL TABLE

Name or Cartridge	Weight in Grains and Brand of Powder (Approximate only)	BULLET			Length of bbl. in arm tested	Muzzle velocity (50 ft. from muzzle)	Energy—foot lbs. Wv²+2g	Penetration (Inches in white pine.)
		Exact diameter in inches	Weight in grains	Round or flat nosed				
Rim Fire:								
.22 Short	1.6 Lesmok	.223	30	RN	6	789	41.5	3
.22 Long	2.1 "	.223	35	RN	6	770	46.2	3½
.22 L. Rifle	3.4 "	.223	40	RN	6	765	51.8	4
.22 W.R.F.	3.5 "	.2275	45	FN	6	811	65.8	4
Central Fire:								
.25 Auto Colt	1.1 Bullseye	.251	50	RN	2	733	59.7	3
7.63 m.m. Mauser	5.5 "	.3105	86	RN	5½	1397	373	11
7.65 m.m. Luger	4.1 "	.3095	93	RN	4½	1173.5	284.3	10
9 m.m. Luger	4.6 "	.3555	125	FN	4	1039.2	299.8	10
.32 W.C.F.	10.0 Sharpshooter	.3125	115	FN	5½	954	232.4	5
.32 Auto Colt	2.5 Bullseye	.3125	74	RN	3½	938	144.8	5
.32 S.&W.	1.5 "	.315	85	RN	4	606.7	69.5	3
.32 S.&W.	1.5 "	.315	85	RN	10	902	159	4
.32 Lg. Colt	2.0 "	.313	90	RN	4	641.4	82.2	3½
.32 Sht. Colt	1.4 "	.315	80	RN	4	657.2	76.7	3½
.32 S.&W. Long	2.0 "	.315	98	RN	4	706.9	108.6	4

Cartridge	grs.	Brand							
.32 Colt N. P.	2.5	"	.314	98	FN	4	706.3	108.6	4
.38 S. & W. Auto	1.9	"	.3195	76	RN	3½	809	110.5	4
.38 S. & W.	2.4	"	.359	145	RN	5	579.3	108.2	4½
.38 Auto Colt	4.6	"	.359	130	RN	6	1175.	398.0	10
.38 Colt N. P.	2.4	"	.359	150	FN	4	579.8	111.7	4
.38 Sht. Colt	2.5	"	.375	130	RN	6	608	107	4
.38 Long Colt	3.0		.358	148	RN	6	788	203	4½
.38 Long D. A.	3.4	Gray Walsrode	.358	150	RN	6	771.6	198.3	8
.38 S. & W. Spl.	3.4	Bullseye	.358	158	RN	6	856.7	257.5	7
.38 Colt Spl.	3.4	"	.358	158	FN	6	857.6	258	7
.38 S. & W. Spl. Gal.	8.5	C. P. W. *	.358	70	RN	6	1300	263	5
.38 S. & W. Spl. Mid. Range	2.1	Bullseye	.358	123	RN	6	655	99	9
.38 W. C. F.	15.	Sharpshooter	.400	180	FN	5	983.	386.5	6
.380 Auto Colt	2.6	Bullseye	.357	95	RN	3½	887	166	5½
.41 Sht. Colt	2.5	"	.406	160	RN	6	707	177	8
.41 Long Colt	3.3	"	.387	200	RN	8	705.6	221.2	8
.44 S. & W. Russ.	4.1	"	.431	246	RN	6	706	272	6½
.44 S. & W. Russ. Gall.	2.5	"	.431	115	RN	6	685	118	3
.44 S. & W. Spl.	5.1	"	.431	246	RN	5	755	311.5	7
.44 W. C. F.	16.5	Sharpshooter	.426	200	FN	7½	918.8	375	6
.45 Auto Colt	4.7	Bullseye	.4505	200	RN	5	910.2	368	8
.45 Auto Colt (Govt.)	4.7	"	.4505	200	RN	5	809	335	6
.45 Colt D. A.	5.0	"	.455	230	RN	5	770.6	336.3	5
.455 Colt	4.5	"	.458	255	RN	5	756.6	336.5	5
.455 Webley Auto	7.0	Cordite	.455	265	RN	5	750	280.6	4½
.455 British Service	5.5	"	.455	265	RN	7½	700	288	4¾

* California Powder Works. This brand of powder is not retailed to small consumers.

CHAPTER 4

Sights

The purpose of sights is to assist in aiming the piece. The national organizations allow only "open" sights in pistol and revolver shooting."Peep" or "aperture" sights are barred. The rear sight usually consists of a notch shaped like a V or a U, the notch being as wide on top as at any part. The front sight is a piece of thin metal set on edge. Sometimes the latter has a special shape or section resembling a pinhead when looking at it from the breech, as in aiming.

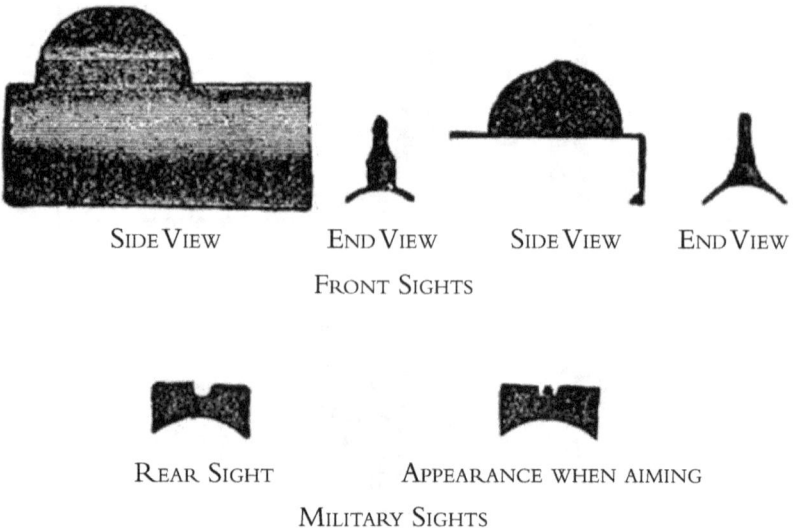

SIDE VIEW   END VIEW   SIDE VIEW   END VIEW

FRONT SIGHTS

REAR SIGHT   APPEARANCE WHEN AIMING

MILITARY SIGHTS

FIGURE 58.

Military sights usually consist of a plain groove in the top of the frame for the rear sight and a tapering front sight fixed to the barrel near the muzzle.

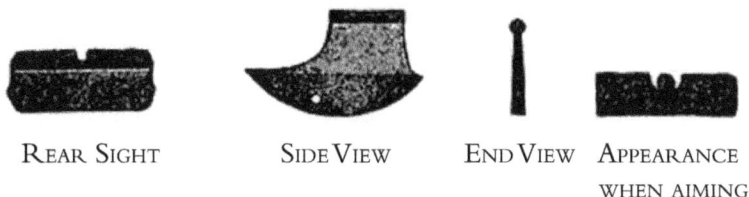

| REAR SIGHT | SIDE VIEW | END VIEW | APPEARANCE WHEN AIMING |

"PAINE" SIGHTS.

FIGURE 59.

Target sights are made in endless variety to suit individual ideas. The sights most generally used for target shooting are the "Paine" sights, named after Chevalier Ira A. Paine, who invented and was the first to use them. The rear sight is a flat bar with a semi-circular notch, and the front sight is a "bead" sight; that is, a sight that resembles a pinhead when aiming.

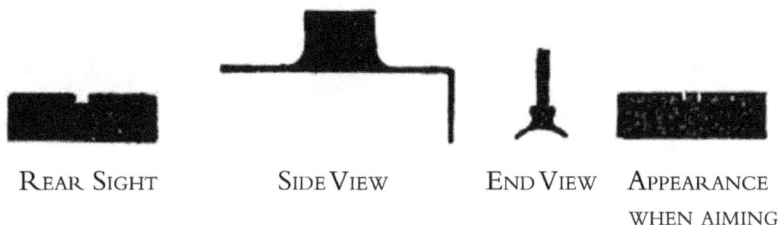

| REAR SIGHT | SIDE VIEW | END VIEW | APPEARANCE WHEN AIMING |

PATRIDGE SIGHTS.

FIGURE 60.

Another sight that many of the best shots are using is the "Patridge" sight, developed by Mr. E. E. Patridge of Boston, Mass. The rear sight has a wide rectangular notch; the front sight is plain, with a square top, as shown.

Fig. 61 represents the "Lyman" sights as adapted to Smith & Wesson revolvers. The distinctive features of these sights are the ivory bead of the front sight and the horizontal ivory line in the rear sight. These sights are well adapted for hunting and shooting at objects with a dark background.

These sights have been referred to in the order in which they are most used. It is generally necessary for individuals to try various sights before they are able to select intelligently. In target arms different-shaped sights may be used in the same base or fitting, so that it is a comparatively easy matter to try any or all of these sights on the same arm.

The notch of the rear sight should have a bevelled edge concave toward the front. This will secure sharpness of outline in any light. The front sight should also be distinct and is found to be more satisfactory when the side toward the eye is a surface at right angles to the line of sight.

FIG. 61.—LYMAN SIGHTS

FIG. 62.—THE WESPI SEARCHLIGHT SIGHT
A-Battery; B-Mercury switch; C-Electric bulb; D-E-Lenses.

FIG. 63.—THE WESPI SEARCHLIGHT MOUNTED ON A POCKET REVOLVER.

50

For years means have been sought to make successful shooting at night possible. White and phosphorescent paints have been applied to the sights and to the top of the barrel but all such methods have proved more or less unsatisfactory even in dim light and in total darkness the target or other object cannot be seen. A recently invented device that overcomes all these difficulties and makes shooting at night practicable is the "Wespi" searchlight sight.[1]

This sight is a tube about 6 inches long and ¾ inches in diameter containing a miniature electric searchlight which projects a dark spot in the centre of the illuminated field. When properly mounted on the piece the black spot indicates where the bullet will strike. This sight can be readily attached to any pistol or revolver. As offered on the market at the present time it is adapted for short range work up to, say, 60 feet. The illustrations show a section through the sight tube, and the sight attached to a revolver. The weight is six ounces. (See Fig. 61 and 62.)

This sight embodies the principles of the telescopic sight and can undoubtedly be modified to increase its illuminating power and adapted so as to project well-defined dark lines similar to cross wires, on a target; or the dark spot decreased in size to about 3 or 4 inches in diameter at 60 feet. So modified this would be a practical sight for target shooting and would be a boon to many of the older marksmen whose sight is failing and who find it more and more difficult to shoot in artificial light with the ordinary sights.

Such a sight would also possess many advantages for beginners as the moving spot on the target would indicate the unsteadiness of the holding and impress upon the marksman the importance of holding the spot in the right position at the instant of discharge. A further improvement would be to substitute for the dark spot, a spot of intensely bright light. This would be equally as effective as the dark spot and would greatly increase the range at which the sight could be used, adapting it to game shooting at night. It is hoped that the manufacturers will develop a sight as suggested for target and game shooting.

---

1. Sold by American Specialty Co., 198 Fifth Avenue, New York City.

CHAPTER 5

Shooting Position

The position in pistol and revolver shooting is very important. In firing a long series of shots, a man with an easy, natural position will suffer much less fatigue, and will have a decided advantage over another whose position is straining and uncomfortable. Formerly the approved position was to stand with the right side toward the target. This required the head to be turned ninety degrees from its natural position, and was very uncomfortable. Undoubtedly this position is a relic of duelling days, when it might have been argued that a smaller mark was offered to the antagonist.

The positions adopted by the leading shots vary considerably. Most of them face a trifle to the left of the target, with the right foot 6 or 8 inches ahead of the left, and pointing directly toward the target, the weight of the body supported equally by both legs and perfectly balanced. Others shoot with the feet close together; some with one or both eyes open, and with the arm partly or fully extended. The question of position depends largely upon the physique and comfort of the individual.

Mr. Winans' position is an exceedingly strong one. His poise is very good, and he stands firmly on both feet. The left arm falls straight down along the left side of the body. This affords rigidity when desired, and imparts action to the figure.

Mr. Axtell has a stanch, natural position. Like Mr. Winans, he shoots with the right arm fully extended, and he holds the weapon in the correct and most approved manner.

The position of Mr. Anderton is excellent. He enjoys perfect health, and has his large muscular development well under control. His position is strong, natural, and comfortable.

Mr. Dietz's position is entirely different from any of those preced-

FIG. 64.—WALTER WINANS FIG. 65.—C. S. AXTELL FIG. 66.—THOMAS ANDERTON

ing. It is tenseless and flexible permitting him to shoot long series of shots without fatigue.

The positions of Mr. Patridge and Sergeant Petty are characteristic and typical of persons of entirely different physique.

Mr. Gorman and Dr. Sayre are men of similar physique. Their positions which resemble each other closely are firm, easy and natural.

Mr. Lane's position is natural and interestingly unconventional. He has perfect poise and shoots without apparent fatigue.

Dr. Snook has a well poised and deliberate position. He shoots with his arm not fully extended and with the feet close together.

The positions of Mr. Armstrong and Mr. Dolfen are very similar. They are men of entirely different stature but almost identical in physique. Their positions are firm and business-like. Both shoot with the arm fully extended.

Note.—For more photographs showing shooting positions of individuals referred to in this chapter, see illustrations also in next chapter.

CHAPTER 6

Target-Shooting

In the development of firearms and ammunition, target-shooting has always occupied an important place. It is regularly and systematically practised in the army and navy, in order to maintain and improve the proficiency of the men as marksmen. Target-shooting, with many different styles of firearms, under prescribed rules and regulations, has also become extremely popular with civilians.

Target-shooting was indulged in extensively with the rifle before it became popular with the pistol and revolver. The shorter barrel, and the greater difficulty in acquiring skill with the latter weapons, were doubtless responsible for the mistaken idea, long prevalent, that these arms were extremely inaccurate. When, however, a few individuals developed sufficient skill to obtain fine shooting, their performances were considered phenomenal.

Among the first to obtain a high order of skill with the muzzle-loading pistol in the United States was Captain John Travers of Missouri. He was well known as an expert pistol shot as early as 1860. In that year Captain Travers shot an interesting individual match in St. Louis at a distance of 100 feet. Fifteen china plates, nine inches in diameter, were used as targets. Captain Travers broke 11 out of 15, while his opponent broke but 9.

In 1865 Colonel William F. Cody, (Buffalo Bill) and Captain William P. Schaaf of St. Louis became prominent as pistol shots. The latter subsequently joined Captain Travers in a three years' tour of the United States, giving exhibitions in nearly all the large cities.

About 1880 Ira Anson Paine, a native of Massachusetts, attracted attention by his fine marksmanship with the pistol. In 1881 he went abroad, and for a number of years he travelled over the principal countries of Europe, giving public exhibitions of his skill with the pistol

FIG. 67.—JOHN A. DIETZ FIG. 68.—E. E. PATRIDGE FIG. 69.—SERGT. W. E. PETTY

and revolver. While in Portugal in 1882 he was knighted by the King in the presence of a notable assemblage, and made a chevalier of an ancient military order.

In his exhibitions Chevalier Paine used a Stevens Lord Model pistol and a Smith & Wesson revolver. His skill with these arms was so far in advance of his contemporaries that he was popularly supposed to accomplish many of his feats by trickery.

Target-shooting with the pistol and revolver, as a sport, may be said to have originated at the annual meeting of the National Rifle Association at Creedmoor in 1886. During that meeting a revolver match was scheduled to be shot at 25 yards on the 200-yard Standard American Rifle Target.

It was a re-entry match, with the three best scores of five shots each of any contestant to count. In this match three scores of 48 out of 50 were made, the highest individual aggregate of three scores being 143 out of a possible 150.

The same year a similar match was announced at the fall meeting of the Massachusetts Rifle Association at Walnut Hill. Chevalier Paine was a competitor in this match, and made 50—49—49==148 in six entries. The next best three scores equalled 142.

These matches proved so interesting and successful that target-shooting with the pistol and revolver became instantly popular all over the country. It was soon found that the arms possessed remarkable accuracy, and as the skill of the shooters improved the distance was increased to 50 yards retaining the same target.

Mr. A. C. Gould, editor of *The Rifle*, and *Shooting and Fishing*, was the first one to recognize the possibilities of the pistol and revolver, and became greatly interested in the performances with these arms. He assisted and encouraged the shooters, witnessed their work, and made careful and elaborate records of all the important scores that were made in the United States from 1886 to 1900. It was at his suggestion that Chevalier Paine essayed to fire the first 100-shot score at 50 yards on the Standard American Target, scoring 791 points. This shooting was done with a finely sighted .44-calibre Smith & Wesson Russian Model Revolver, regulation full charge ammunition, and a 2½-pound trigger pull. A keen rivalry for the 100-shot record soon sprang up, resulting as follows:

Oct. 15, 1886, Chevalier Ira Paine at Walnut Hill			....	791
March 7, 1887, Chevalier Ira Paine "	"	"	....	841
Nov. 4, 1887, F. E. Bennett "	"	"	....	857
Nov. 14, 1887, F. E. Bennett "	"	"	....	877
Dec. 5, 1887, F. E. Bennett "	"	"	....	886
Dec. 17, 1887, Chevalier Ira Paine "	"	"	....	888
Dec. 22, 1887, Chevalier Ira Paine "	"	"	....	904
Dec. 23, 1887, W. W. Bennett "	"	"	....	914

This rivalry led to a long newspaper controversy, and culminated in the famous Paine-Bennett revolver match. The conditions were as follows: Stakes $1000.00; 100 shots per day for six consecutive days; Smith & Wesson Russian Model Revolvers, .44 calibre; factory-loaded full charge ammunition; trigger pull, 3 pounds; Standard American Target with 8-inch bullseye; distance, 50 yards. On the fifth day of the match, and while 9 points in the lead, Chevalier Paine entered a protest and withdrew. Mr. F. E. Bennett continued shooting, as stipulated in the match, scoring 5093 points for the total of the six days. The protest was referred to the National Rifle Association, which decided in favour of Mr. Bennett, awarding him the match and the championship of America.

In practising for this match Mr. F. E. Bennett, under the same conditions, made a score of 915. This record was not excelled until June 1, 1901, when C. S. Richmond of Savannah, Georgia, scored 918 points under substantially the same conditions.

During the summer of 1890, Mr. William E. Carlin, assisted by Mr. Hubert Reynolds, made a very elaborate series of tests with the revolver and various kinds of ammunition, to ascertain the possibilities of the arms, the accuracy of the ammunition, the effect of fouling, etc. About 10,000 rounds were fired, Mr. Carlin used a butt-stock attachment, telescopic sight, and sand bag rest; and Mr. Reynolds verified Mr. Carlin's results from a machine rest. All the shooting was done with black powder charges in Smith & Wesson revolvers.

The best groups were made with the .32-44 S. & W. Revolving rifle cartridge; a number of the 10-shot groups at 50 yards, measuring 1¼ inches to 1½ inches in diameter. Tests were also made at ranges of 100 and 200 yards. At 100 yards, groups of 10 shots were obtained with the .32-44, and the .44 calibre S. & W. Russian, varying from 3 inches to 4 inches in diameter. At 200 yards, the .44 S. & W. Russian gave the best results; a number of groups of 10 shots being obtained measuring 8 inches to 12 inches in diameter. These tests were considered most remarkable at that time, as such accuracy was not expected of barrels of only 6 inches and 8 inches in length.

Prior to these tests, the possibilities of the pistol and revolver were judged solely by the shooting of a few expert shots, which of course included the personal dispersion error of the individuals. These tests furnished the first definite information as to the real capabilities of the revolver, and had a far-reaching and salutary influence on pistol and revolver shooting. They demonstrated to the marksmen and the manufacturers of the arms that fine shooting approximating to that of the rifle was possible with the revolver, by developing the necessary skill in shooting and perfecting the ammunition.

A very interesting revolver match for a trophy offered by Mr. Walter Winans took place in 1892. Mr. Winans is a noted American revolver shot, residing in England, and the trophy—an American cowboy executed admirably in bronze—was modelled by him. The match was conducted by *Forest and Stream*. The trophy was won, after a spirited competition, by Doctor Louis Bell. Under the conditions of the match, the winner was to defend his title two years before the trophy became his property. The trophy was won successively by George E. Jantzer and Sergeant W. E. Petty. Sergeant Petty defended the trophy successfully for two years, and now holds it permanently.

A record, or "best on record," is the highest recognized score of any given number of shots fired under certain standard conditions, and with an arm complying with certain established rules. The records of pistol and revolver shooting in the United States were carefully established and compiled by *Shooting and Fishing* until the year 1903.

The record performances with the single-shot pistol, on the Standard American Target, at 50 yards, are as follows:

100 SHOTS—

Sept. 22, 1888, F. E. Bennett, Walnut Hill, Mass.....	906
Nov. 10, 1888, F. E. Bennett " " "	934
Sept. 10, 1890, F. E. Bennett " " "	936
Feb. 25, 1900, J. E. Gorman, San Francisco, Cal.....	939
May 26, 1901, J. E. Gorman " " "	942
March 1, 1902, E. E. Patridge, Walnut Hill, Mass.....	942

50 SHOTS—

Nov. 10, 1888, F. E. Bennett, Walnut Hill, Mass.....	470
Feb. 11, 1900, J. E. Gorman, San Francisco, Cal.....	471
May 20, 1901, J. E. Gorman " " "	474
Dec. 7, 1901, T. Anderton, Walnut Hill, Mass.....	476
April 4, 1903, T. Anderton " " "	480

Fig. 70.—J. E. GORMAN Fig. 71.—R. H. SAYRE Fig. 72.—A. F. LANE

Under the stimulating influence and encouragement of *Shooting and Fishing*, pistol and revolver shooting became a popular pastime and by 1900 numerous clubs had been organized throughout the country. Unfortunately, the marksmen of each locality made their own rules and adopted independent standards as to targets, weapons, etc. This resulted in endless confusion and dissatisfaction when matches between clubs were attempted. Rumours of a challenge from the revolver marksmen of France for an international contest were also rife at this time. There was, therefore, an urgent need for a national organization to exercise general jurisdiction over the sport; formulate uniform rules, regulations, and standards, and to receive and act upon challenges.

A number of revolver enthusiasts met in Conlin's shooting gallery, New York City, in February, 1900, and issued a call to the revolver shots of the country, inviting them to join in forming a national revolver association at a meeting called at Conlin's gallery, March 5, 1900. Replies were received from thirteen states and thirty-five gentlemen responded in person to the invitation. The United States Revolver Association[2] was organized at that meeting.

This association, with the support and co-operation of all the leading shots of the country, immediately assumed national jurisdiction, formulated rules to govern pistol and revolver shooting, and inaugurated the annual championship matches. These are shot simultaneously in different parts of the United States, thus giving everybody an opportunity to enter the competitions.

The influence of the association on pistol and revolver shooting has been very beneficial. It has established uniformity in arms, rules, etc., and has encouraged and conducted many friendly matches between clubs, thus bringing the shots in different parts of the country in closer touch with each other.

The most important activity of the association in recent years has been the inauguration of the Indoor League Matches. Clubs in all parts of the United States enter into an agreement to shoot a match with each club in the League during the winter season. Medal prizes are awarded by the association according to the percentages of matches won to matches shot, similar to baseball leagues. The League has become exceedingly popular and twenty to thirty clubs participate in the contest annually. The League agreement varies somewhat from year to year. The 1914 agreement will be found in the Appendix.

2. See Appendix for Constitution, Annual Matches, Rules and Regulations, etc.

Fig. 73.—J. H. Snook Fig. 74.—George Armstrong Fig. 75.—P. J. Dolfen

International Matches.—The U. S. Revolver Association also negotiates and conducts all the international matches. The first of these matches was between France and the United States and took place on June 16, 1900. This match attracted world-wide attention, and was won by the United States. The conditions of the match were as follows; Ten men on a side; the Americans to shoot at Greenville, N. J., and the Frenchmen in Paris. Results to be cabled. Each side to appoint an umpire to witness the shooting of the opposing side. Each man to shoot 30 shots on the French target at 16 meters and 30 shots on the Standard American target at 50 yards.

Following are the complete scores of the members of both teams on the two targets:

FRENCH TEAM—	On French Target	On American Target	Grand Total
M. Dutfoy	244	253	497
Comte de Chabannes	240	250	490
M. M. Faure	241	248	489
Paul Gastinne	238	251	489
Comte Clary	247	241	488
Capt. Chauchat	243	241	484
Com. Dilschneider	236	242	478
P. Moreau	239	236	475
M. Trinité	233	239	472
M. Labbé	226	240	466
Totals	2387	2441	4828

AMERICAN TEAM—	On French Target	On American Target	Grand Total
J. A. Dietz	263	260	523
W. E. Petty	259	252	511
R. H. Sayre	253	251	504
B. F. Wilder	239	263	502
G. W. Waterhouse	253	246	499
L. R. Piercy	244	241	485
W. G. Hudson	222	250	472
J. B. Crabtree	225	244	469
W. A. Smith	224	240	464
A. L. A. Himmelwright	228	232	460
Totals	2410	2479	4889
Americans led by	23	38	61

The first match did not satisfy the revolver experts of France, who claimed that the French team was not national in its character, that instead of representing the whole of France it represented Paris alone. About June, 1902, it was suggested that a second international contest be held, and the French gentlemen began at once to gather material for a representative team. The army, the navy, and the revolver and pistol clubs of France united in their efforts to organize as strong a team as possible.

The conditions of the second match were the subject of considerable negotiation by correspondence and as finally agreed upon were as follows:

Fifteen men on a side. Each man to shoot 60 shots in 10 strings of 6 shots each on the Standard American Target at 50 yards. Each side to appoint two umpires to witness the shooting of their opponents. Results to be cabled.

The American marksmen assembled at the Walnut Hill range of the Massachusetts Rifle Association, near Boston, devoting three days to preliminary practice shooting and selecting the team. It was originally agreed upon that the match was to take place on June 30, 1903, and the American team shot their scores on that day. Owing to delays in transportation, the targets intended for the French team did not reach them promptly and their side of the match was shot several days later. The members constituting the teams and their respective scores are as follows:

FRENCH TEAM

Comte de Castelbajac. Libourne	547
Commandant Py, Saint Omer	542
M. Dutfoy, Marseilles	541
Captain Moreaux, Rennes	529
M. Moline-Paget, Dieppe	526
Captain Chauchat, Versailles	524
M. Keller-Dorian, Lyons	522
M. Feugray, Paris	509
M. Despassio, Lyons	503
M. Lecocq, Paris	502
M. Caurette, Ham	502
M. Louvier, Paris	496
M. Balme, Paris	469
Adjutant Paroche, Rennes	466
M. Sartori, Paris	462
Team total	7,640

AMERICAN TEAM

O. I. Olson, Duluth, Minn	554
B. F. Wilder, New York, N. Y	543
R. S. Hale, Boston, Mass	540
J. A. Dietz, Jr., New York, N. Y	534
W. A. Smith, Springfield, Mass	532
C. S. Axtell, Springfield, Mass	530
Louis Bell, Boston, Mass	527
T. Anderton, Boston, Mass	523
J. B. Crabtree, Springfield, Mass	519
I. R. Calkins, Springfield, Mass	519

E. E. Patridge, Boston, Mass.................... 517
R. H. Sayre, New York, N. Y. (Score shot in
  Paris....................................... 515
J. T. Humphrey, Boston, Mass................. 513
W. S. Amory, 2d, Boston, Mass............... 512
C. L. Bouvé, Boston, Mass.................... 511

   Team total 7,889
   Americans led by.......................... 249

A careful analysis of the scores shows that the Americans shot much more evenly than the Frenchmen, and that the skill of the three high men on both teams was approximately equal.

The next international match participated in by the revolver shots of the United States was the Olympic Games Match at London, England on July 10 and 11, 1908. Preliminary and elimination trials were conducted under the auspices of the United States Revolver Association resulting in the selection of the following team: I. R. Calkins, Springfield, Mass.; C. S. Axtell, Springfield, Mass.; J. A. Dietz, New York, N.Y.; and J. E. Gorman, San Francisco, Cal.; R. H. Sayre, New York, N.Y., Captain. The conditions of the match were as follows:

Any revolver or pistol with open sights; any ammunition; trigger pull unrestricted; distance, 50 yards; international target, 10 ring, 2 inches in diameter, rest of target divided by concentric rings one inch apart, bullseye containing 10, 9, 8, and 7 rings; 60 shots in strings of 6 shots; 2 sighting shots allowed; position standing, right or left hand with arm extended; maximum number of entries from any country in individual contests, 12; maximum number of entries from any country in team contest, 1; teams to consist of four men each.

A time limit of four minutes for each string of five shots was established, and all other conditions of the matches were governed by the rules of the National Rifle Association of Great Britain.

The result of the match was as follows:

   1st—United States:
        J. E. Gorman 501
        I. R. Calkins 473
        John A. Dietz 472
        C. S. Axtell 468
                                            ——— 1914

   2d —Belgium 1863
   3d —United Kingdom 1817
   4th—France 1750
   5th—Sweden 1732
   6th—Holland 1637
   7th—Greece 1576

65

The next Olympic Contest was held at Stockholm, Sweden, in 1912. The American team consisted of A. P. Lane, New York, N. Y.; H. E. Sears, Boston, Mass.; P. J. Dolfen, Springfield, Mass.; and John A. Dietz, New York, N.Y.; R. H. Sayre, New York, N.Y., Captain.

The match was shot on July 2nd, under practically the same conditions as the former Olympic Match and resulted as follows:

```
1st—United States:
        A. P. Lane .............................. 509
        H. E. Sears ............................. 474
        P. J. Dolfen ........................... 467
        J. A. Dietz ............................ 466
                                              —— 1916

    2d —Sweden ........................................ 1849
    3d —United Kingdom ............................... 1804
    4th—Russia ....................................... 1801
    5th—Greece ....................................... 1731
```

In the individual match which was shot on July 1st under the same conditions, and participated in by over fifty competitors of the different nations, Mr. Lane and Mr. Dolfen won first and second places with scores of 499 and 474 respectively. Mr. Sears won 7th place with a score of 459, and Mr. Dietz 9th place with a score of 454.

CHAPTER 7

Targets

A target is a mark or object of suitable form and colour designed to be fired at. It usually consists of a frame covered with canvas or paper, presenting a white surface with a prominent spot or bullseye in the centre. Concentric circles or "rings," around the centre divide the target into zones which are assigned values, decreasing from the centre outward. On a regularly equipped range the targets are movable frames, so arranged that they may be raised to the firing position and then lowered into a pit, where the marker can safely examine the target, mark the shot accurately, and cover the shot-hole with a paster. The sum of the values of a limited series of consecutive shots, as 5, 7, 10, 20, 50, etc., constitutes a score.

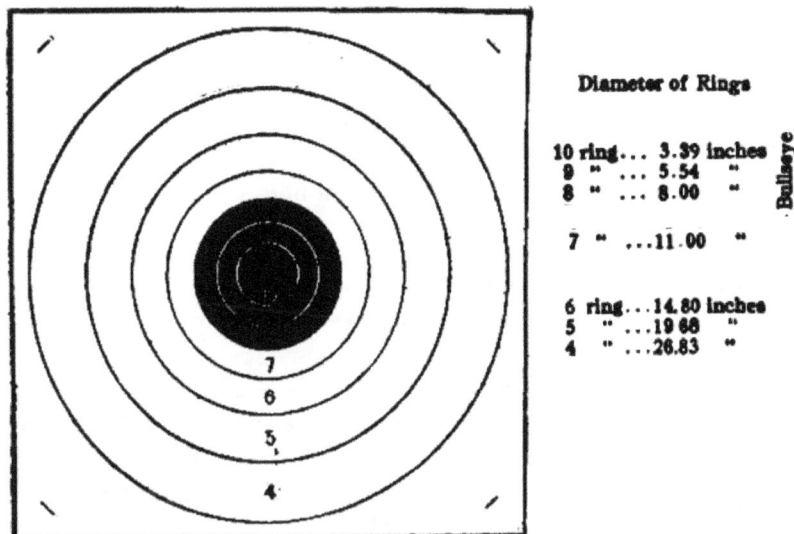

Diameter of Rings

10 ring... 3.39 inches
9 " ... 5.54 "
8 " ... 8.00 "

7 " ...11.00 "

6 ring...14.80 inches
5 " ...19 68 "
4 " ...26.83 "

Bullseye

FIG. 76—STANDARD AMERICAN TARGET

The official target of the United States Revolver Association, which is used in the annual championship matches and for record shooting, is the Standard American Target.

This target is used by practically all the shooting clubs and organizations in the United States. For 50-yard shooting the bullseye is 8 inches in diameter and contains the 8, 9, and 10 rings. This target is well suited for target practice at this range. It has been used extensively since 1886. Ten shots, with one hundred for the possible, usually constitute a score.

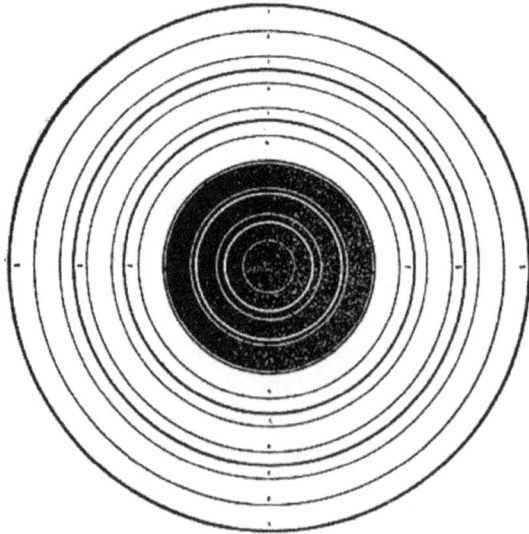

FIG. 77—THE U. S. R. A. COMBINATION TARGET.
(Standard American rings in heavy lines and
International in light lines.)

This target as supplied by the United States Revolver Association for use in all the outdoor championships shows also the rings of the International Union target (in light lines) and is known as the "Combination" target.

The International target rings do not interfere in any way with the shooting or the scoring by Standard American count, and they have the distinct advantage that the marksman may easily determine, for purposes of comparison, what any score is by International count.

FIG. 78—THE INTERNATIONAL UNION TARGET.
Diameter of 10 ring==5 Centimetres==1.9568 ins.
Other rings==2½ Centimetres, about 0.984 in.
Diameter of 1 ring==50 Centimetres==about 19¾ in.

The International Union Target is used in the Olympic Games Matches, and has been adopted by nearly all the European and South American countries for pistol and revolver contests at 50 meters. It is without doubt the best target for the purpose in general use. The ten-ring represents approximately the average dispersion of the most accurate revolvers and pistols and with the concentric rings a uniform distance apart, the score has a proper relation to the dispersion of the shots. The size of the target, about 19¾ inches in diameter, is also well determined. The target could be improved by increasing the size of the bullseye so as to include the 6 ring. This would make sighting on it less straining and would improve the scores. The target so modified would be better adapted for the United States Revolver Association Matches than the one now used.

Target L is the Regulation Pistol Target used in the prescribed target practice of the War Department. It is used also in the National Pistol Match.

For gallery shooting at 20 yards the Standard American Target is reduced so that the bullseye is $2^{72/100}$ inches in diameter, and for 10-yard shooting 1 inch in diameter.

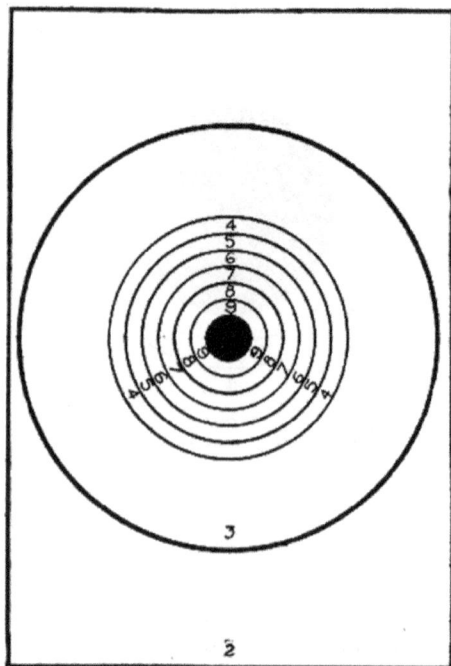

FIG. 79—TARGET L. (U. S. ARMY.)
Diameter of bull's-eye counting 10==5 Ins.
Concentric rings around it, 9, 8, 7, 6, 5, and 4, are 1¾ ins. apart.
Diameter of 4 ring==26 ins. Diameter of 3 ring==46 ins.
Rest of target, 4ft. x 6ft. Counts 2.

An arm of large calibre has a decided advantage over one of small calibre in short-range shooting, on account of the larger hole made by the bullet, and, for this reason the large calibres are preferred for gallery shooting. For distances less than 25 yards not more than five shots should be fired on a paper or cardboard target. In case a close group is made, the scoring will be much easier and more accurate than when ten shots are fired at a single target.

The best grades of target arms are capable of making "possibles" or perfect scores on the Standard American Target, using regulation ammunition. To make high scores is therefore simply a question of skill on the part of the shooter.

A great many other targets designed principally for rifle-shooting have been recommended at different times by well-known and scientific marksmen. Some of these targets possess much merit and have become popular in certain localities. It is unquestionably a mistake to introduce new targets in this manner as long as satisfactory targets are in general use, and on which all the important matches and records have been shot. The merit of a score on a new target cannot be judged by those unfamiliar with it, and frequently a highly meritorious score fails to receive the recognition it deserves on account of having been shot on a comparatively unknown target.

In selecting a target for longer ranges than 50 yards it is always preferable to have the bullseye sufficiently large so as to be seen with ease and comfort when sighting. Small bullseyes strain and tire the eyes and have no advantage whatever.

In England and France the targets generally have smaller bullseyes than here. At Bisley, the shooting is principally at a distance of 20 yards on a bullseye 2 inches in diameter. At 50 yards the bullseye is 4 inches in diameter. The English targets have no circles of count within the bullseye. The regulation targets of the United Shooting Societies of France have bullseyes 5 and 6 centimetres in diameter for the pistol and revolver, respectively, at 20 meters, and 20 centimetres in diameter for 50-meter shooting. All these targets have two or more circles of count within the bullseye.

CHAPTER 8

Target Practice

In order to become familiar with the arms and develop skill in shooting, careful and systematic practice is necessary. This can be most conveniently and intelligently obtained in target-shooting. At a properly equipped range, each shot is "spotted"[1] as fired, so that the shooter can tell instantly where each shot strikes. This is a great aid and advantage, as it enables the shooter to note the effect of changes in light, wind, slight displacements in sights, etc., and modify his work accordingly. The usual distance is 50 yards in the outdoor matches and 20 yards in the indoor contests.

Very good shooting has been done at 100 yards, and even at 200 yards, but such long-range shooting is rarely attempted except by the very best shots. The whole target being so small at that distance, a shot need not be very wild to miss the target. Such an occurrence is very unsatisfactory and disconcerting even to a fairly skilful shot. There is, moreover, nothing to be gained by extremely long-range work. The pistol and revolver are not designed for it, and there is much more pleasure and satisfaction at the shorter ranges.

It is customary and desirable to practise at the target under conditions governing the annual championship matches. This accustoms one to those conditions, and is a decided advantage if one expects to enter the competitions. It is also excellent training for record shooting. In target practice with military arms, regulation full-charge ammunition should be used in all cases, especially when practising rapid-fire shooting. With target weapons, reduced charges are frequently used,

---

1. The position of a shot accurately indicated by a marker from a pit or safe place near the target. A disc of sufficient size to be seen easily from the firing point attached to the end of a pole is used for this purpose, the marker placing the disc over the shot hole for a few seconds immediately after each shot is fired.

and the shooting is generally slow and deliberate.

Target practice is required in all the branches of the military and naval service of the United States. This practice varies somewhat from year to year both in character and amount. The recent adoption of the magazine pistol as the service weapon by the War Department has resulted in a number of changes in the regulation target practice, the conditions and details of which are fully explained in the *Small Arms Firing Manual* for 1914.

The *Manual* also details a prescribed course of target practice for the Organized Militia, which includes the National Guard of the various states. This is adapted principally to the revolver, as the National Guard has not yet been armed with the regulation automatic pistol. As fast as the latter is issued, the organized militia will adopt the target practice prescribed for the army with the regulation weapon.

The revolver until 1915 was the service weapon of the United States Navy, but it has now been superseded by the automatic pistol (Colt, Government Model, .45 cal.). The 1917 firing regulations are novel and drastic, in some respects are much more elastic than those formerly in effect, and are very practical. They are published in a pamphlet of 62 pages.

A digest of all the foregoing target practice will be found in the Appendix.

Matches and Competitions.—Various matches and competitions have been established under the auspices of the recognized shooting organizations which not only give an opportunity of testing the skill of individuals and teams but also, by the scores made in successive years under the same conditions, indicate the improvement and advance in the sport. Most of these matches or competitions are annual events. The International Matches at the Olympic Games take place every four years.

The conditions of the annual championship matches of the United States Revolver Association are excellent and the experience of fourteen years since they have been instituted proves that they are well adapted to stimulate interest in the sport, improvement in the arms and ammunition and develop a high order of marksmanship. The matches are conducted simultaneously in many places throughout the United States under the supervision of authorized representatives and under as nearly identical conditions as possible.

In connection with these matches re-entry matches under the

same conditions are provided which furnish preliminary practice for competitors who wish to enter the championship events. The League contest which is conducted by this association affords excellent practice indoors, and enables the marksmen to keep In good form during the winter months.

The "National Pistol Match" is an annual event conducted by the National Rifle Association of America. It is specially interesting and instructive as it affords an opportunity for civilians to compete in the same contest with the best shots in the Army, Navy and National Guard.

The conditions, prizes, and complete details of all these annual matches will be found in the Appendix.

From time to time special contests are arranged such as the Pan American Matches held at Camp Perry, Ohio, in 1913, the International Shooting Festival to be held at San Francisco in 1915 during the Panama Fair, etc. The matches of such special meetings often vary in their conditions. Special prizes are provided for the occasion.

CHAPTER 9

Revolver Practice for the Police

The revolver is a part of the regular equipment of the police force of nearly every city in this country. Unfortunately the general lack of any regulations for the care of and the practice with these arms largely nullifies their usefulness. Even in the large cities, members of the police force frequently admit that they have not used or cleaned their arms for six months or more. An inspection of the arms under such conditions not infrequently reveals the fact that centre-firearms are loaded with rim-fire ammunition, and *vice-versa*. The mechanism is often so badly rusted that the cylinder will not revolve and the barrel so corroded as to seriously impair its accuracy. When occasion requires the use of the arms under such conditions, accidents almost invariably result, either to the policemen who attempt to fire the arms, or to the innocent bystanders and property.

The records of every large municipality show that large sums are annually disbursed in litigation and to individuals who have suffered either personal wounds or property damage from accidents of this character.

By adopting suitable arms, and regulations governing practice shooting with them, it is entirely practicable and comparatively easy to train a large police force to become good marksmen. The possibility of accidents is thus reduced to a minimum and the efficiency of the men increased to a maximum. The moral effect of a high order of marksmanship of an entire police force, when generally known, cannot be overestimated. Practice and skill in the use of the revolver embodies the essential elements of rifle shooting, so that in case of riot, insurrection, or war, a large police force could be made quickly available for duty with very little additional instruction, by arming them with rifles.

75

A practical plan to develop such results is as follows: The services of a competent person to teach the men must first be secured. This man should be an experienced and skilful marksman with the revolver and be qualified to maintain proper discipline and teach the subject in all its details. A suitable range must next be provided. Two men from each precinct selected for their fitness to become instructors should then be detailed to take a prescribed course of training and practice under the teacher referred to. Each of these men should devote not less than four hours a week to this course. In four months' time these men should be qualified to undertake the work of training and instructing others under the inspection and supervision of the original teacher. After providing sufficient range facilities, squads of men from each precinct should then be detailed for practice and instruction under their own instructors, devoting at least two hours per man per week to this work. At least one and one-half hours of this time should be devoted to actual practice shooting. After sufficient skill has been developed, teams of the different precincts should shoot matches with each other, which will keep up a friendly rivalry and promote interest in their work.

By adopting such a plan it is possible, within a year from its inception, to convert an entire police force into perfectly safe and reliable shots of good ability; i. e., such ability as would enable all of them to hit an object the size of a man every time at 50 paces. The mistake is sometimes made of requiring the men to practice during off-duty time; this has never proved successful.

After the first year, or after a sufficient degree of skill has been developed, the efficiency of the men can be preserved and maintained by devoting an hour every two weeks to regulation practice. There is little doubt but that the cost of the time and ammunition devoted to such a course of training would be more than offset by the elimination of a large portion of the accidents, litigation, etc., that result under the present conditions.

Much of the efficiency that it is possible to attain depends upon the character of the regulation arm that may be adopted for police service. Such an arm should be of large calibre and sufficient power to fulfil the requirements. When carried in the pocket the perspiration of the body causes rust, and a nickel finish will therefore generally be more serviceable than any other. The sights, hammers and other projections should be of suitable form, and as referred to in the text under "Pocket Arms." In order to secure suitable accuracy, the barrel should be 4 inches in length and the trigger pull 4 pounds. A first-class weapon for police service is the .38-calibre Smith & Wesson safety hammerless, the .38-calibre or .32-calibre Colt Police Positive or the .32 calibre Smith & Wesson hand ejector revolver. The .38-calibre Smith & Wesson safety hammerless is particularly well adapted for police service, the safety feature making accidental discharge almost impossible, and being also a decided advantage in case the weapon should fall into the hands of an unskilled antagonist.

In all cases a regulation arm and ammunition should be adopted so as to secure uniformity and involve the purchase of only one line of supplies and ammunition.

The following course of instruction and regulations for practice shooting are recommended:

REVOLVER PRACTICE

Regulations.—All members of the department are obliged to practice shooting with the regulation arm, at least two hours in each calendar month. The captain of each precinct will designate the time and place for instruction and practice for each individual under his jurisdiction.

Every member of the department will be expected to qualify in one of the three classes: Marksman, Sharpshooter, or Expert, and will be rated accordingly. Decorations of suitable design will be awarded to those qualifying; the decoration to be worn directly under the shield. Ratings in any year will be determined by the average scores made by each individual in the three months prior to January first of that year, on which date decorations will be awarded annually. A member failing to qualify in any class shall be rated a beginner, and if holding a decoration awarded the preceding year shall surrender same.

All practice shooting shall be in the prescribed order in each class as given below. Entries unlimited. Each individual must qualify at each stage before he can be advanced to the next stage. All shooting to be done under the following:

General Conditions. The position shall be standing, free from any support, the weapon being held in one hand with the arm extended so as to be free from the body. Target, standard American 200-yd. rifle target with 8-in. bullseye, outside dimensions 28½ in. by 28½ in. Ammunition shall be the regulation full charge, factory loaded, brought to the firing point in the original package. Arms shall not be loaded except at the firing point, when the competitor is ready to shoot his score. All scores to be 10 shots, fired in two strings of 5 shots each. Slow fire to be timed after the first shot of each string. Rapid fire to be timed as follows: The competitor standing at the firing point with the arm loaded, not cocked, and the barrel pointing downward in a direction not less than 45 degrees from the target, when ready to begin each string shall say, "Ready." The scorer, watch in hand, when the second hand reaches an even 10-second point on the dial, will give the command "Fire," *after which* the competitor raises and cocks his weapon and begins his string. Just as the time limit for each string expires the scorer shall announce, "Time."

If a shot is fired after the time limit has elapsed, the shot of highest count shall be deducted from the string. In case of misfire, accidental discharge, or defective ammunition, it shall be scored as a shot and if the bullet does not strike the target it shall be scored zero. Ties and all other details not covered by these conditions to be decided by and to comply with the Rules and Regulations of the U. S. Revolver Association.

MARKSMAN COURSE

Slow Fire:—10 shots at 10 yds. One minute for each string of five shots. Possible, 100; qualifying score, 90.

Rapid Fire:—10 shots at 10 yds. 30 seconds for each string of five shots. Possible, 100; qualifying score, 80

SHARPSHOOTER COURSE

Slow Fire:—10 shots at 20 yds. One minute for each string of five shots. Possible, 100; qualifying score, 90.

Rapid Fire:—10 shots at 20 yds. 30 seconds for each string of five shots. Possible, 100; qualifying score, 80.

EXPERT COURSE

Slow Fire:—10 shots at 20 yds. 30 seconds for each string of five shots. Possible, 100; qualifying score, 90.

Rapid Fire:—10 shots at 20 yds. 15 seconds for each string of five shots. Possible, 100; qualifying score, 80.

Inasmuch as regular instruction and practice in revolver shooting has been instituted in only a few of the larger cities of this country, the police of other cities in the absence of such training, or its equivalent, have so little knowledge as to the proper use and care of the revolver that the arm adds little or nothing to their efficiency. To assist such policemen individually who have the ambition to increase their efficiency by their own initiative, the following practical suggestions and general rules will prove helpful:

General Rules and Instructions

Never point a revolver in any direction where it would do harm if it went off accidentally. *Always observe this rule* whether the arm is loaded or not.

In carrying the loaded revolver on the person see that the hammer rests between two cartridges. (Or if of the rebounding hammer type have one chamber of the cylinder empty and opposite the hammer.)

When necessary to use the revolver on vicious dogs, etc., such animals should be driven into a rear yard or alley where there is soft ground to stop the bullets. Never shoot on the sidewalk or a paved street where it can be avoided, on account of the liability of the bullet glancing off and doing serious damage. Similarly when firing to attract attention, shoot into soft ground or a heavy timber, when practicable, instead of into the air.

Never attempt to shoot while running. Stop for a moment and take deliberate aim. The shots will then be effective.

Thoroughly clean and oil the revolver as soon after using it as practicable. If carried on the person regularly it should be overhauled and re-oiled inside the barrel and cylinder as well as outside, once a week, to keep it in good condition.

In case regular practice shooting is not provided when on duty, practice target shooting when off duty, firing at least 50 shots once a month and following the prescribed course as given in this chapter as near as possible.

CHAPTER 10

Pistol Shooting for Ladies

The great majority of ladies have some inherent dread of all varieties of firearms. This is no doubt largely due to the senseless and ir-
resistible desire of inexperienced persons to indulge in a mock-heroic
display and flourish of such arms when in the presence of ladies. All
useless demonstration and ostentation with fire arms serves only to
distinguish those who are unfamiliar with their proper manipulation
and use. Persons handling arms in this manner should be avoided, or
promptly compelled to desist. Many of the accidents of the "I did not
know it was loaded" order occur in this manner.

There is nothing occult or mysteriously dangerous about fire arms,
but their potential power must never be forgotten in handling them.
As a weapon of defence the revolver places the weakest and most di-
minutive person skilled in its use, on an equality with the most powerful antagonist. Ladies who travel extensively and visit semi-civilized
countries, especially the wives and daughters of men in the diplomatic
service and of the army and navy officers assigned to foreign stations,
should be thoroughly familiar with fire arms and skilled in their use.

The necessity of knowing how to shoot, like knowing how to
swim, may occur but once in a woman's lifetime, but when occasion
does require either, it is generally under circumstances involving peril
to life, and for that reason both are advantageous and valuable accom-
plishments. Every woman should, therefore, be sufficiently familiar
with fire arms to know how to handle them safely, and, in emergency,
to use them with intelligence. While skill in the use of the pistol and
revolver is a useful accomplishment, the practice of shooting with
these arms will prove exceedingly interesting. Target practice with the
.22-calibre pistol is particularly well suited for ladies, and those who
have the opportunity to indulge in it have invariably found it an en-

joyable and fascinating pastime. There is every reason, too, to believe that ladies would excel and develop a higher order of skill in pistol shooting than gentlemen, because they are generally more temperate and possess a more delicate nervous system.

A number of civilian shooting clubs have successful ladies' auxiliary clubs. There are at the present time a large number of ladies who are skilful markswomen with the pistol and revolver.

Any of the target pistols referred to in the text under the subject of arms (except the Remington pistol, which is a very heavy piece) are suitable for ladies' use. A very serviceable and handsome combination is furnished by Smith & Wesson, which consists of their regular target pistol with a 10-inch barrel and an interchangeable .38-calibre revolver barrel and cylinder, fitting to the same stock. These are furnished in a special case with cleaning rods, etc., making a complete and attractive set. The .22-calibre Smith & Wesson Hand Ejector with a 6-inch barrel and .22-calibre Colt Police Positive Target revolvers are also well adapted for ladies' use.

It is well to begin practice with a .22-calibre pistol, as this is a light and very pleasant charge to shoot, and the tendency to "flinch" is reduced to a minimum. After a fair degree of skill has been developed with the .22-calibre pistol reduced charges with a revolver may be tried and from this stage the practice shooting can progress to the regulation full charges. It is desirable that ladies should have a little practice with the revolver with full charged ammunition, so as to be able to manipulate it with sufficient confidence and skill in case of necessity.

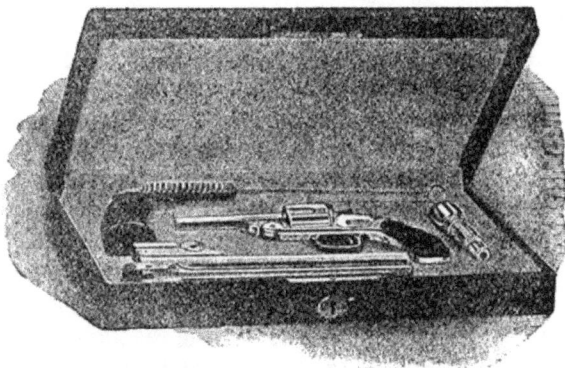

Figure 80.
Combination Set.—Smith & Wesson .38-Cal. Revolver, .22-Cal. Pistol, Utensils, etc., in Case.

CHAPTER 11

Clubs and Ranges

(For a complete detailed description of range construction, including illustrations, practical working drawings, etc., the reader is referred to *Rifle Range Construction*, published by the E. I. du Pont Powder Company, Rifle Smokeless Division, Wilmington, Del.)

Whenever three or more persons in any locality are interested in rifle or revolver shooting, a club can generally be organized and additional members secured. If the business affairs are properly and conservatively managed, much pleasure will result for the members at a nominal cost. Approximate ideas of the cost of constructing and maintaining ranges and indoor "galleries" can generally be obtained by communicating with the officers of existing clubs. In preparing the Constitution and By-Laws, that of the United States Revolver Association will be an excellent guide.[1] The secretary-treasurer of that association will be able to give valuable assistance to new clubs.

The first requisite of a shooting club is a suitable range. A 50-yard range adapted to pistol and revolver practice can be constructed at a comparatively small expense. At the firing point a room or house should be provided with booths at least three feet wide with openings facing the targets. A substantial butt must be supplied behind the targets to stop the bullets, including the wildest shots. This should be an earthen embankment, or may be a natural uninhabited hill with a steep slope toward the range. The range should be measured and laid out by an engineer, or other competent person using a steel tape.

A pit at least 8½ feet deep should be dug for the safe accommodation of the markers, and provided with a safely shielded side entrance. The uprights and other target framing should set against the back

---

1. See Appendix.

side of this pit. The width of the pit from the framing toward the firing point should be 5 feet, and the length should be made about 3½ feet for each set of alternating targets. The alternating target frames to which the targets are to be attached may be of wood with heavy canvas stretched over them. The frames should be at least 30 inches square and should be so arranged that they can easily be moved up and down between the vertical posts in grooves or slides, like "double-hung" window sash, and so as to balance each other by means of cords running over pulleys located in the posts at about the height of the bottom of the target when in its highest position, the cords being attached to the lower corners of the frames.

They should be so adjusted that when one target is at the top and in position to be fired at, the other is at the bottom of the pit. Over each set of alternating targets and attached to a cross piece at the top of the uprights should be placed large numbers from 3 to 10 inclusive, for marking each target. A roof or shelter should be erected so as to shade the target and keep out the rain. Suitable timbers or steel plates should be provided to protect the slides or grooves between the targets from damage by wild shots. Steel plates are sometimes placed a short distance behind the targets, slanting forward at the top, to positively stop the majority of the bullets, but these must be far enough behind the targets or inclined sufficiently so that the spatter of lead will not injure the men in the pit. If possible, have the targets so located that they are due north of the firing point.

Such a range is operated as follows: A marker is sent into the pit for each target to be operated; paper targets having been pasted to the canvas on the frames a sufficient length of time previously so as to be dry. The marker pulls down one of the targets which raises the other into the firing position. As soon as the shot is fired, the marker, using a 10-foot rod with an iron disc 2½ inches in diameter fastened on the end as a pointer "spots" the shot by placing the disc over the bullet hole, and then pointing to one of the numbers over the target corresponding to the value of the shot. The disc on the pointer should have one side painted white so that it can be easily distinguished when covering shots in the bullseye.

The scorer at the firing point then scores the shot as indicated by the marker. The marker then raises the target at the bottom of the pit in position for the next shot, which brings the first target down into the pit where the marker covers the bullet hole with a paster. This operation is repeated for each shot.

FIGURE 81.
Details of alternating targets, pit, etc., for 50-yard range.

Where a score of ten consecutive shots is to be made on each paper target without covering the bullet holes with pasters, as in the United States Revolver Association Matches, the target is fastened to the frame with double pointed carpet tacks and left in the firing position until the ten shot score is completed, each shot being "spotted," marked, and scored as fired. When the score is completed, another paper target having been placed on the alternating frame in the pit, the latter is raised promptly ready for the next score.

In large cities it is often necessary to provide a suitable range for target shooting indoors and by artificial light. Such a range is designated a "gallery." The standard range is 20 yards for the revolver and pistol, and 25 yards for the rifle. The arrangement at the firing point is practically the same as in the case of the 50-yard ranges, the booths being at least 3 feet wide. On account of the small size of the target and the short distance, it is feasible to move the target back and forth, from the firing point to the butt by "trolleys" operated by a hand wheel, the latter being located generally at the left hand side in the booth at the firing point.

The "trolley" carriage consists of a heavy steel spring clamp holding a cardboard target (about 9 inches square) at the top edge of the target, the carriage being supported by a No. 8 or 10-gauge wire stretched from the firing point to the butt, at a level of about 2 feet above the line of fire. The supporting wires are attached to the wood-work at the firing point by means of eye-bolts, which also regulate the tension of the wires. The trolleys are operated back and forth by an endless braided cord passing around angles over pulleys screwed to the wood-work of the booth, and around the hand wheel. A steel plate with the lower part inclined away from the firing point 20 or 30 degrees is placed about 12 inches back of the targets to stop the bullets and prevent them from gouging out the wall or wood-work behind. By deflecting the plates as described, the spatter of lead is directed downward, and thus prevents damage to the wood-work around the targets. A suitable background behind the targets may be provided by white or light gray paint, or by a suitable fabric.

If the splatter of the bullets mars the targets, a shield of 1-inch boards can be erected and maintained between the target and the steel plate.

The lighting may be accomplished by a line of gas jets or electric lights about 2 feet in front of the targets and at the same distance either above or below them. At least two jets should be used to light

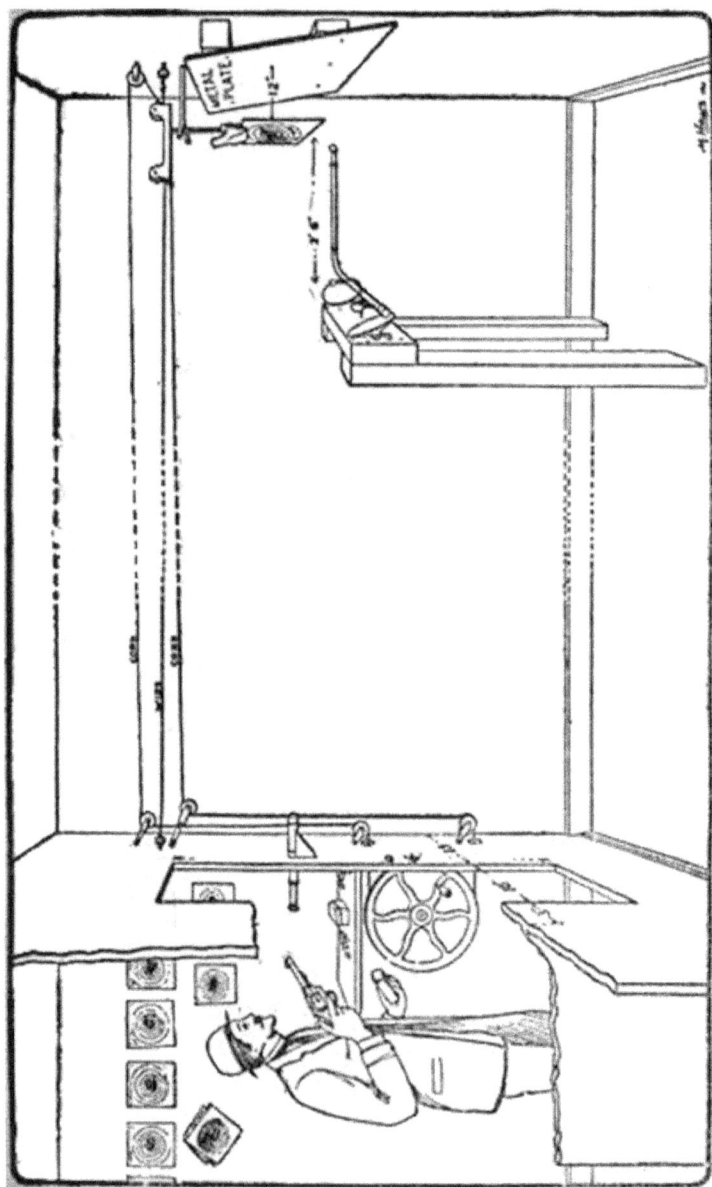

FIGURE 82.

Details of booths at firing line, "trolleys," and butt for gallery ranges.

each target, otherwise the flicker of the gas jets makes the light unsatisfactory. The reflectors should be of tin or other metal, polished or painted white. Glass is too fragile for this purpose. Heavy timbers or steel plates must be provided to protect the lights and piping from wild shots. A telescope is mounted in each booth to enable the marksman to see the location of shots in the bullseye.

When floor space is limited the rifle ranges can sometimes be located over the revolver ranges, or the latter, if the range is in a cellar, may be depressed by constructing a pit of a suitable depth at the firing point. The booths for rifle shooting and the operation of the targets are practically the same as already described.

It is best to complete all the work at the target end of the range first. After the location of the targets is definitely fixed the position of the firing line can be determined by making the distance from the target to the firing point two inches in excess of 20 yards or 50 yards as the case may be. The slight excess distance does not affect the shooting appreciably, but it is important in order to avoid any possibility of having scores disqualified in case the range should be questioned and later be checked or verified and found "short." It is desirable whenever possible to have the ranges of the standard lengths especially if matches with other clubs are contemplated.

The table for cleaning arms, and for tools, should never be placed near the booths, but on the opposite side of the room, to avoid congestion at the firing line.

The floor on which the contestants stand at the firing line must be firm and solid, so as not to vibrate or move when others walk about in close proximity. A concrete floor covered with a carpet or rug of firm texture is excellent.

In indoor shooting smokeless powder and reduced charges are always to be preferred. When artificial ventilation is provided, some shooting may be done with black powder ammunition, but the range soon fills with smoke, rendering the targets indistinct and the atmosphere unpleasant. Gallery practice is very valuable, as it enables one to preserve good form in the winter months, in localities where it is too cold to shoot with comfort and pleasure out-of-doors.

The following simple rules should be printed and posted in conspicuous places in every shooting range or gallery:

RULES

Arms shall be unloaded until the contestant is at the firing point.

Loaded arms shall be handled with the muzzle pointing toward the targets.

Automatic arms shall be used only under the personal direction of the Shooting Master.

Contestants are requested to use the greatest care in handling arms at all times.

The authority of the Shooting Master in charge shall be absolute.

The rules of the United States Revolver Association shall govern all match shooting.

The above rules must be strictly observed and will be enforced.

The Walnut Hill Range of the Massachusetts Rifle Association is one of the best 50-yard revolver ranges in the country, (as at time of first publication). A well-equipped gallery of up-to-date design is that of the Crescent Athletic Club, Brooklyn, N.Y.

FIG. 83.

Shooting Gallery of the Crescent Athletic Club, Brooklyn, N.Y.

CHAPTER 12

Hints to Beginners

(Under this subject the author aims to give helpful practical information and advice for the benefit of all who wish to acquire skill in
pistol and revolver shooting.)

Selection of Arms.—There is no single arm that can be used advan-
tageously for all classes of shooting. It is therefore necessary in the
first place to decide for what purpose the arm is to be used. A careful
perusal of the text under "Arms" and "Ammunition," will be of assistance in reaching a decision. The next step is the selection of the arm.
As already stated, the cheap, unreliable, and unsafe arms are to be carefully avoided. It is preferable to buy a second-hand arm of a reputable
manufacturer, if in good condition, than a new one of inferior make.
Second-hand arms frequently have defects that cannot be detected by
the novice, and, if obliged to buy a second-hand arm, it is advisable
to ask some expert shot to assist in making the selection. The price
of the best grades of pistols and revolvers is, fortunately, within the
reach of almost every one, and, if at all possible, new arms should be
purchased.

In any case, whether a new or a second-hand arm is to be chosen,
it is well to examine and handle all the different models of the best
makers. The fit and feel of the arm are very important. Select an arm
that feels comfortable, and which, when properly held, fits the hand so
that the first joint of the trigger finger just touches the trigger when
that part of the finger is bent at right angles to the barrel.

The correct manner of holding the pistol or revolver is shown in
Fig. 84 and illustrates how the hand should fit the arm. Note particularly the position of the trigger finger and the thumb. The trigger finger in this position acts directly backward in pressing the trigger, and
the thumb assists materially in steadying the piece. If the piece is too

large for the hand, the trigger finger will be more or less extended, and will pull side-wise to a greater or less degree, and thus increase the difficulty of fine shooting. Fig 84a illustrates the approved position of the thumb when the locking catch interferes with the extended thumb. The fit of the arm is much more important, and has a vastly greater effect upon the results than fine distinctions between the merits of the different arms.

Any of those named are excellent and are capable of shooting much more accurately than they can possibly be held by the most expert shots. A man with a large hand will probably find the Remington pistol or the Colt New Service revolver best suited for him; another with a hand of medium size will find the S. & W. pistol or the S. & W. Russian Model revolver most desirable; while another still, with a small hand, may prefer the Stevens pistol or the .38-calibre military revolver, either the S. & W. or the Colt.

If an arm is wanted for steady use, select the plain blue finish, and wood handles; elaborate engraving and gold, silver, copper, or nickel finished arms are handsome and pleasing, but, if much used, become burnt and discoloured where the powder gases escape, and soon become unsightly. A blued finish is also to be preferred when shooting in the sunlight. Most arms as offered on the market have hard rubber handles. These become smooth and slippery when the hand perspires, and are not as desirable as wood handles. A few expert shots prefer pearl handles.

The trigger pull should have the smallest possible travel and be smooth and positive. The smaller the travel of the hammer and the more rapid its action, the quicker will be the discharge after pulling the trigger. If the trigger does not pull smooth and "sweet," or becomes "creepy" from wear, it should be corrected by a skilled gunsmith. While the rules allow a trigger pull of 2 pounds for the pistol and 2½ pounds for the target revolver, many expert shots prefer to have their arm pull from ½ to 1 pound more. The rules also allow 7½ and 8 inch barrels for the revolver. Many of the experienced shots prefer to have their revolvers balance near the trigger, and are of the opinion that the extra length of barrel above 6½ inches does not offset the disadvantage of poorer balance. In the pistol, however, the length of the barrel is invariably 10 inches. Accuracy in aiming is lost very rapidly as the distance between the sights is reduced below 7½ inches.

For target shooting, the .22-calibre pistols will be found admirably

FIG. 84.—CORRECT MANNER OF HOLDING THE REVOLVER
WITH THUMB EXTENDED

FIG. 84 A.—SHOWING THUMB WHEN LOCKING CATCH
INTERFERES WITH EXTENDED POSITION

suited for beginners. The charge being light, there is less liability to "flinch," a fault easily and most invariably acquired when the novice begins shooting with a heavy charge. The practice in aiming and pulling the trigger with these arms is excellent training and a first-rate and valuable preliminary to the more difficult and practical work with the revolver.

The double-action feature in a revolver is of very little practical value. Owing to the varying amount of resistance to the trigger in operating the mechanism, the aim is disturbed more than if the hammer is cocked with the thumb. Even in rapid-fire shooting better results are obtained with a double-action arm if used as a single action. It is also more difficult to make the trigger pull smooth and short in double-action mechanisms.

Manipulation.—Most of the accidents with firearms are caused by carelessness and ignorance in manipulating them. The revolver and pistol, being much smaller, are more dangerous to handle than the rifle or shotgun. An experienced pistol shot can easily be singled out by the extreme care and unostentation with which he handles his arms.

On picking up an arm, or if one is handed to you, open the action at once and make sure it is not loaded. *Always* do this, even if it is your own arm and you are quite sure it was not loaded when you last put it away; some one, without any idea of danger, may have loaded it in your absence. Cultivate and practise the habit of always holding the arm, whether loaded or unloaded, so that it points in a direction where it would do no harm if it were to go off unexpectedly.

By observing these simple rules, serious accidents will be impossible. No one should be allowed to handle firearms in a shooting club or participate in any of the public matches until these rules have been thoroughly mastered.

Position and Aiming.—If you know of a club or shooting organization to which one or more first-rate pistol and revolver shots belong, it is well to join it, if possible. Much more rapid progress can be made by observation and by following the suggestions of experienced shots than if one is obliged to solve the various problems without such assistance or advice. In order to familiarize yourself with your arm, it is well to practise aiming and pulling the trigger before any actual shooting is attempted. By inserting an empty shell for the hammer to strike upon, the piece may be aimed and "snapped" without injury.

The position you adopt is very important. Stand firmly on both feet, with the body perfectly balanced and turned at such an angle as is most comfortable when the arm is extended toward the target in aiming. Let the left arm assume any position that may be comfortable and natural. Select a small black spot with an extensive white background to sight at. A small black paster on a window-pane with the sky for a background, is excellent for this purpose. When the aiming is correct, that is, when the sights are properly aligned, their position with reference to the spot or bullseye should be as shown in Fig. 85. The top of the front sight should just make contact with the lower edge of the bullseye corresponding to the position of 6 o'clock. It has been found by experience that it is less fatiguing to lower the arm, fully extended, holding the piece, to the target than to raise it up to the target.

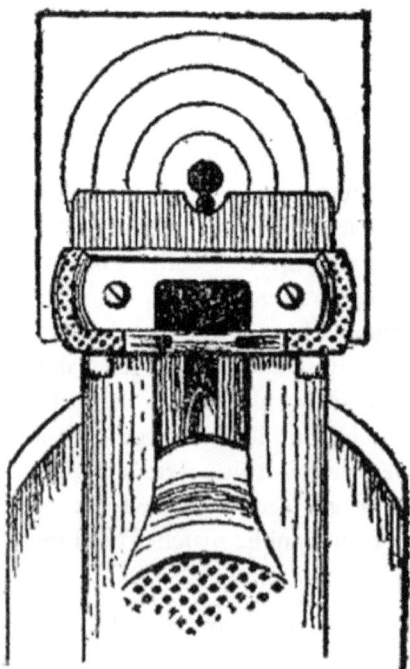

FIG. 85—CORRECT POSITION OF THE SIGHTS IN AIMING AT THE TARGET.

Firing.—With the pistol or revolver in the right hand cock the hammer with the thumb, making sure that the trigger finger is free from the trigger and resting against the forward inner surface of the trigger guard. In cocking the piece have the barrel pointing upward. Then extend the arm upward and forward, so that when you assume your firing position the piece will point about twenty degrees above the bullseye. With your eyes fixed on the bullseye at 6 o'clock inhale enough air to fill the lungs comfortably and lower the piece gradually until the line of the sights comes a short distance below the bullseye. Now, holding your breath and steadying the piece as well as you possibly can, bring the line of sights into the position shown in Fig. 85. At the same time gradually increase the pressure on the trigger directly backward, so that when the sights are pointing at the bullseye the hammer will fall.

Be careful not to pull the trigger with a jerk, but ease it off with a gentle squeeze, so as not disturb the aim. Accustom yourself not to close the eye when the hammer falls, but note carefully where the line of the sights actually points at the instant that the hammer falls. You will, no doubt, find it almost impossible to pull the trigger at the moment the sights are just right. The hammer will fall when the line of sights may point a little too high or too low, or to one side or the other of the bullseye; but patient practice will correct this, and in time you will be able to let off the arm at the right moment.

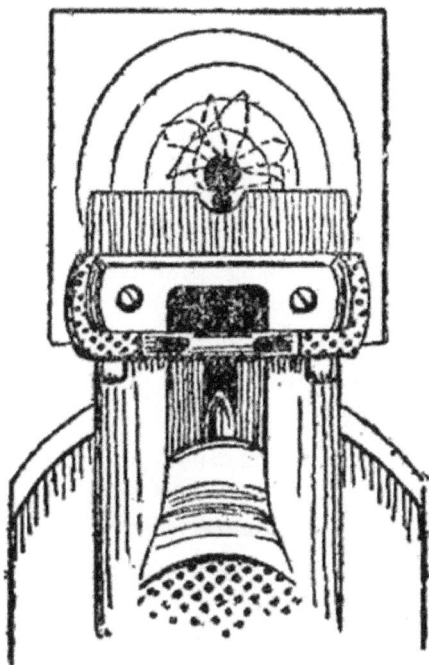

FIG. 86—SHOWING THE TRAVEL OF THE LINE OF THE SIGHTS ABOUT THE
BULLSEYE IN AIMING

95

The pulling of the trigger is a very delicate operation; it is, in fact, the most important detail to master—the secret of pistol and revolver shooting. If the trigger is pulled suddenly, in the usual way, at the instant when the sights appear to be properly aligned, the aim is so seriously disturbed that a wild shot will result. To avoid this, the pressure on the trigger must always be steadily applied, and while the sights are in line with the bullseye.

It is, of course, impossible to hold the arm absolutely still, and aim steadily at one point while the pressure is being applied to the trigger; but, in aiming, the unsteadiness of the shooter will cause the line of the sights to point above the bullseye, then below it, to one side of it, and then to the other, back and forth and around it, as shown by the dotted lines in Fig. 86. Each time that the line of the sights passes over the bullseye the smallest possible increment of additional pressure is successively applied to the trigger until the piece is finally discharged at one of the moments that the sights are in correct alignment. Long and regular practice alone will give the necessary training of the senses and muscles to act in sufficient harmony to enable one to pull the trigger in this way at the right moment for a long series of shots. A "fine sympathy" must be established between the hand, the eye, and the brain, rendering them capable of instant co-operation.

After obtaining a fair idea of aiming, etc., watch carefully when the hammer falls, and note if it jars the piece and disturbs the aim. If not, you are holding the arm properly. If the aim is disturbed, you must grip the arm tighter or more loosely, or move your hand up or down on the handle, or otherwise change your method of holding the piece until your "hold" is such that you can snap the hammer and the aim remain undisturbed. This aiming and snapping drill is largely practised by expert shots indoors, when they do not have the opportunity to practise regularly out-of-doors.

Target Practice.—If your first actual shooting is done at the range of a club, it is best to ask one of the members to coach you until you get accustomed to the rules, etc. A target will be assigned to you, and you will repair to the firing point and load your arm. It is well to let your coach fire the first shot or two, to see if your piece is sighted approximately right. If so, you are ready to begin shooting. If the sights appear to be as in Fig. 85 at the moment of discharge, then the bullet should hit the centre of the bullseye. If, after several shots, you are convinced that the bullet does not strike where it should, the arm is not properly sighted for you.

In adjusting the sights you will find it an advantage to remember a very simple rule: To correct the rear sight, move it in the same direction as you would the shots on the target to correct them, or move the front sight in the opposite direction. Most target arms have the front sight non-adjustable, and the rear sight adjustable for both windage and elevation. A few arms have interchangeable or adjustable front sights for elevation. Move the sights a little at a time, according to the foregoing rules, until they are properly aligned. A few ten-shot scores should then be fired for record. As you become accustomed to the range, rules, etc., you will feel more at ease. This will inspire confidence, and your shooting will improve correspondingly.

Do not have your sights too fine. Fine sights are much more straining on the eyes, and have no advantage over moderately coarse sights. The rear sights as generally furnished are purposely made with very small notches, so as to enable individuals to make them any desired size.

It is well to have the trigger pull at least ¼ of a pound greater than the minimum allowed by the rules. If much used, the pull sometimes wears lighter; and if there is little or no margin, you run the risk of having your arm disqualified when you wish to enter an important match.

Never use other ammunition in your arm than that for which it is chambered. A number of accidents and much difficulty have resulted from wrong ammunition. In the same calibre the actual diameter of the bullets frequently varies considerably, and a few shots, even if they should not prove dangerous, may lead the barrel, and thus cause much delay and annoyance. When a barrel is "leaded" from any cause it will become inaccurate. In such cases, particles of lead usually adhere to the inside of the barrel at or near the breech. A brass wire brush, of suitable size to fit the barrel, will generally remove it. When this fails, carefully remove all oil, cork up the opposite end of the barrel and fill it with mercury, letting the latter remain in the barrel until the lead is removed.

Occasionally the powder is accidentally omitted in loading a cartridge. When the primer explodes, the bullet may be driven partly through the barrel and remain in it. When this happens, whether from this cause or any other, always be careful to push the bullet out of the barrel before firing another shot. If the bullet is not removed, and another shot is fired, the barrel will be bulged and ruined. This may occur with a light gallery charge.

When shooting the .22-calibre long rifle cartridge, there will be an occasional misfire. In withdrawing the cartridge the bullet will stick in the barrel and the powder spill into the action. To prevent this, hold the barrel vertically, with the muzzle up, and withdraw the shell carefully. Then remove the bullet in the barrel with a cleaning rod; or extract the bullet from a new cartridge, inserting the shell filled with powder into the chamber back of the bullet and fire it in the usual manner.

Do not use BB caps in any pistol that you value. They are loaded with a composition of fulminate of mercury in combination with other substances that cause rusting and the bullets have no lubrication. These caps will ruin a barrel in a very short time. The .22-calibre conical ball caps are loaded with black powder, and the bullets are lubricated, making this a much better cartridge; but it is best to adhere to the regular .22 ammunition for which the arm is chambered.

Never under any circumstances shoot at objects on the heads or in the hands of persons. There is always a possibility of something going wrong, and such risk to human life is unjustifiable, no matter how skilful you may be.

It is necessary to exercise extreme care in practising with the pocket revolver. Some persons delight in practising quick drawing from the pocket and firing one or more shots. This is dangerous work for the novice to attempt. Most of the pocket weapons are double action. If the finger is on the trigger and the arm catches in the pocket when drawing, a premature discharge is likely to result, which is always unpleasant and sometimes disastrous. Practice in drawing the revolver from the pocket or holster should always be begun with the arm unloaded. Only after a fair degree of skill is acquired should actual shooting be attempted. For quick drawing from the pocket the only double-action revolvers that are fairly safe to handle are the S. & W. Safety Hammerless, and the Colt "Double Action," which has a safety notch for the hammer to rest on.

Drawing a revolver from a holster is easier and much less dangerous than drawing it from the pocket. Larger and more practical arms are generally carried in holsters, and such arms should be single action in all cases. In practising with a holster weapon, fasten the holster on the belt, and anchor the belt so that the holster will always be at the same relative position. The holster should be cut out so that the forefinger can be placed on the trigger in drawing. Always carry a loaded revolver with the hammer resting on an empty chamber or between two cartridges.

In the woods, or in localities where such shooting would not be likely to do any harm, it is good practice to shoot at a block of wood drifting down in the current of a swift-flowing stream, at a block of wood or a tin can swinging like a pendulum, from horseback at stationary and moving objects, and from a moving boat at similar objects. Such practice is largely indulged in by cowboys, ranchmen, and others in the western part of the United States. The shooting is generally rapid-fire work with heavy charges at short range, and is to be commended as being extremely practical.

Many of the published reports of wonderful shooting are gross exaggerations. The prowess of the so-called "Gun Men" of New York and other large cities is greatly over-estimated. These criminals do not practice shooting with the fire arms they use but operate by stealth and intrigue which makes them dangerous. They are, in fact, very poor marksmen, few of them being able to hit an object the size of a man more than 15 or 20 feet away.

In shooting a long series of shots with black powder ammunition, when the rules allow it, the barrel should be cleaned and examined every six or ten shots, depending upon the clean-shooting qualities of the ammunition used. It is well to examine the shells, also, and note if the primers have been struck in the centre. If not, then some of the mechanism is out of line, and the parts likely to have caused the trouble must be cleaned.

After securing good, reliable arms, stick to them. Much time and progress is frequently lost by buying and trying different arms, ammunition, etc. If in any of your shooting, you should get results that are peculiar and unsatisfactory, make it your business to find out the cause of the difficulty, and remedy it as soon as possible.

"Blazing away" a large quantity of ammunition carelessly and recklessly is absolutely valueless as practice, and is a waste of time. Give your whole attention to your work, and try your very best to place every shot in the centre of the bullseye.

It is very important to keep a full, detailed record of all your shooting, for comparison, study, etc. A suitable book should be provided for this purpose. Do not fall into the habit of preserving only a few of the best scores; but make it a rule to keep a record of *every shot*, and figure out the average of each day's work. The more painstaking and systematic you are, the more rapid will be your progress. By careful, intelligent work, it is possible to become a fair shot in three or four months, and a first-rate shot in a year.

Matches and Competitions.—After a number of good shots have been developed in any club there is generally a desire to measure skill with the members of another club. This leads to friendly matches, which are usually very enjoyable and instructive. Shooting in a match places a man under a certain strain which affects individuals quite differently; some become nervous and shoot poorly when the best work is expected of them, while others are braced up by the occasion and shoot more brilliantly than under ordinary conditions.

Before competing in any match be sure to *thoroughly familiarize yourself with all the conditions.* This will prevent mistakes that frequently disqualify competitors and lead to disagreeable controversies. Avoid getting into any arguments or disputes with range officers, or officials in charge of the matches, and particularly while the matches are in progress. The range officers are invariably extremely busy and it is unjust to the other competitors to usurp more of their time than is your proper portion. They are generally intelligent men who have been selected because of their fitness for the positions they hold, and their decisions and rulings should be accepted as final. If for good cause you should wish to protest against any decision or ruling of an officer in charge, do it in a quiet and gentlemanly way, and whether the rules require it or not, such protest should be made in writing.

Beginners, as well as those who keep up their practice shooting, should enter the annual championships of the U. S. Revolver Association each year. These events are conducted by the Association in different parts of the country simultaneously, under as nearly identical conditions as possible. By this arrangement, long and expensive journeys to one place of meeting are avoided, and all those interested in the sport can participate without serious inconvenience.

Competing in these events is extremely advantageous and beneficial. It enables the beginner not only to note his improvement from year to year, but affords training and experience in shooting under real match conditions, and will correct any misinterpretation of the rules. The more experienced shot, by entering these contests is enabled to compare his skill with that of the leading marksmen of the country, and accurately determine his position among them from year to year.

Persons wishing to compete in the annual championships should practice regularly throughout the year under the conditions of the matches; firing the full number of shots and *within the specified time limits* in all cases.

The National Pistol Match and the National Rifle Association matches are generally held at some selected state or government range, and at a certain specified time. All the contestants are, therefore, shooting on the same ground and approximately under the same conditions. All these matches are shot in the open; i. e. without shelter or protection from the wind. When shooting under these conditions in the glaring sunlight, it is a decided advantage to wear suitable, coloured large-lensed spectacles to temper the light and rest the eyes. The sights and top surfaces of the barrel should be smoked or blackened to prevent the reflection of light. This may be accomplished by burning a small piece of gum camphor, which makes an excellent smoke for this purpose, or by painting with "sight black." A wide brimmed hat will also add to the shooter's comfort in the bright sunlight. Nailed or rubber soles for the boots or shoes are to be preferred because they do not wear slippery.

In squadded competitions the weather conditions must be accepted as they are at the time of the shooting. In re-entry and individual matches the time of the shooting is sometimes optional with the competitor. When this is the case it is a decided advantage to select a time when the conditions of light, wind, etc., are most favourable. On normal clear days, the early forenoon, or just before sunset, are generally the most favourable for suitable light. The wind generally slacks up to a certain degree also just before sundown. Immediately after a shower the conditions are sometimes excellent.

The position of the target with reference to the sun must also be taken into consideration. It is generally best to shoot directly toward or directly away from the sun. Rapid-fire shooting in a gusty wind is perhaps more difficult than under any other conditions. When the wind is steady one can brace up against it and do fair shooting, but when it is unsteady there will invariably be some wild shots. In deliberate untimed shooting one can wait for a lull and get the shots in during such brief intervals.

In practising rapid-fire shooting, great care is necessary in order to prevent accidents, especially in the case of the automatic pistols, which remain cocked and ready to pull the trigger after each shot. In shooting within a time limit, practise to use the entire period and endeavour to do the best possible work, getting in the last shot just before the end of the period.

101

In team matches always follow the instructions and suggestions of your team captain implicitly. Co-operate with him to the limit of your ability in developing the best and most consistent work of each member of the team. Always remember that the high *average* shooting of a team wins more matches than the brilliant shooting of an individual.

In training for matches be abstemious and maintain good physical condition. If your liver is torpid it must be stimulated. Do not tire yourself with too much practice shooting. One or two hours practice daily is generally ample.

Cleaning and Care of Arms.—To maintain the highest efficiency in an arm, it is necessary to keep it in perfect order. The working parts must be kept clean and oiled, and the barrel should receive special attention and care. The residue of some powders is less injurious than that of others, but the arm should in all cases be cleaned and oiled immediately after it has been used. The cleaning should be thorough. Heavy cotton flannel is excellent for this purpose. It should be perfectly dry. Much of the fouling will rub off without moisture, but if moisture is necessary to soften the fouling in places, use thin oil. Never use water, ordinary kerosene, or similar fluids. For certain kinds of smokeless powders, cleaning fluids have been prepared that give good results. Be careful to use the special fluid that is adapted to the particular powder used, as the wrong fluid may not accomplish the desired results.

A good cleaning fluid for many of the Nitro Powders, such as "Bullseye," "R. S. Q.," "Walsrode" etc., is Dr. Hudson's nitro solvent formula, as follows:

Astral oil (or Kerosene free from acid)	2 fluid ounces
Sperm oil	1 fluid ounce
Acetone	1 fluid ounce
Turpentine	1 fluid ounce

Note.—To make sure that the kerosene or Astral oil is free from acid, it can be shaken up with some washing soda, which will neutralize any free acid that may have been present.

To clubs, or those who wish to make up a cleaning fluid in quantities, the above will prove very effective and inexpensive.

For cleaning the inside of the barrel a wooden rod is best. It should have a knob on the end of such size that one or two thicknesses of the cotton flannel around it will fit the bore snug and tight. Square patches of suitable size may then be cut in quantities and used as required. Clean from the breech end of the barrel whenever possible. The slightest burr or injury at the muzzle will spoil the accuracy of an otherwise good barrel. Particular care should be exercised, especially if a steel rod with a slot is used, to prevent the wad from "jamming" in the barrel. Continue cleaning the inside of the barrel until tight-fitting patches, when withdrawn, show no discoloration, and the barrel is warm from the friction of the cleaning. Then saturate a fresh patch with good oil and pass it through the barrel several times, making sure that the entire surface of the grooves has been thoroughly coated with oil. After the cylinder and other parts are cleaned, they should also be oiled.

A good oil for cleaning is "Three in One"; for preventing rust, use Winchester Gun Grease or refined sperm oil. Plenty of oil should be kept on the circle of teeth in which the pawl engages in revolving the cylinder. If smokeless ammunition is used, the oil should be removed from the interior of the barrel and the chambers of the cylinder, a day or two after the first cleaning, and fresh oil applied.

In warm weather, when the air is humid, arms rust very quickly. If they are not kept in an air-tight compartment, they should be inspected, and, if necessary, re-oiled every few days. Under favourable conditions, a thorough cleaning and oiling will preserve the arm in good condition for a month.

If it is desired to store the arms, or protect them for long periods of time, the interior surfaces of the frame, and all the mechanism, should be carefully cleaned and oiled, and then the entire space within the frame filled solid with non-liquid grease, like the Winchester "gun grease." After cleaning the barrel and cylinder, the bore and chambers in the cylinder should be filled solid with the grease. This treatment excludes the air, and absolutely prevents oxidation. The exterior should be oiled, and then coated heavily with "gun grease." Place the arm in a dry woollen cloth, or flannel cover, and wrap it up in a double thickness of new manila paper of the weight of ordinary writing paper. Repeat this, wrapping twice more, each wrapping independent of the other. Then lay the arm in a dry place, where the temperature will always be uniform, and not so warm as to melt the grease. An arm protected in this way will remain in good condition for a period of two years.

Another method of protecting weapons from rust is to immerse them in oil. The wood or rubber stocks should be removed and the arms suspended from a rack in a large glass jar with a ground glass cover to prevent the evaporation of the oil. This is a very quick and effective method and is much more convenient than the preceding plan. The best quality of refined sperm oil should be used.

Chapter 13

Reloading Ammunition

The factory-loaded ammunition for pistols is so excellent that little is to be gained by hand loading. It is sometimes desirable, however, to use special loads that are not furnished by the factories, and such ammunition must be loaded by hand. Then, too, many persons prefer to reload ammunition for economical reasons. In order to do this successfully, considerable experience and skill are necessary. The first attempts at reloading are invariably unsatisfactory and disappointing, and sometimes result disastrously. Extreme care and close attention to details are absolutely essential, especially if smokeless powders are used. It is much the safest and best plan for those who are unfamiliar with reloading to observe and study the methods used by skilled persons, and, if possible, have their first work supervised by an experienced person.

Primers.—The primers are made of copper and brass and are adapted for either black or smokeless powders. The primers for pistol and revolver cartridges are made more sensitive than for rifle cartridges. If, by mistake, rifle-cartridge primers are used, there are likely to be many misfires. The original pasteboard boxes in which the cartridges or shells are purchased invariably have labels designating the kind of primer that should be used in reloading them.

The quality of the primers affects the results to a much greater degree than most persons imagine, especially in reduced or gallery charges. In handling or in transportation the priming composition is sometimes loosened, dropping out of some of the primers and leaving them considerably weaker than the rest. On opening a new box, empty it carefully, and if any appreciable quantity of loose priming is found, the primers should not be used for ammunition intended for fine shooting.

Shells.—The shells are generally made of brass with a solid head containing a pocket for a primer. There is considerable variation in the thickness of the metal from which shells are made by the various manufacturers. Since the outside dimensions must be the same in order to fit the chamber, it follows that the inside diameter of the shells will vary. When the shell is to be crimped a slight difference in the size is unimportant, but for fine target work using black powder, it is preferable not to crimp the shell. In the latter case the bullet must fit sufficiently tight so that it will not be dislodged by the recoil of the arm.

The size of the bore, when adapted to the same cartridge, varies a trifle, also, with different manufacturers. With the slight difference in the size of the shells it is therefore generally possible to select a make of shell the size of which will be just right to hold snugly in position by friction a bullet that exactly fits the bore of the arm. These refinements in the fit of the bullet and shell are important in securing good results with reduced loads.

In pistol and revolver shooting, the shells may be reloaded many times with smokeless powders. The small charge and the consequent reduced pressure do not seem to render the shells brittle and unsuitable for reloading, as is the case with the shells of many of the high-pressure rifle cartridges.

Bullets.—In the large ammunition factories the bullets are made by the swaging process, with heavy machinery. They are, in consequence, very uniform in density and size. They are packed in boxes of twenty-five and fifty and are lubricated ready for use. While very few persons are able to mould bullets as good as those factory-made, when bullets of a particular shape, weight, or temper are desired, they must be moulded.

The Ideal Manufacturing Company's dipper and melting pot[1] are useful for this purpose. The best quality of lead in bars or pigs should be used. If the bullets are to be hardened, "block tin," which may be had at any hardware store is alloyed with the lead. Weigh the proper quantity of each metal to give the desired proportions. Melt the lead in the pot over a steady fire and then add the tin. At this stage add a small quantity of tallow or beeswax to the molten metal (about the

1. The Ideal Manufacturing Company (Marlin Firearms Co., successors) of New Haven, Conn., publishes a handbook containing full information in regard to moulding bullets, reloading ammunition, tables, and other useful information relating to shooting.

size of a .45-calibre round bullet) and stir briskly with the dipper. This will flux the mixture and make it flow better. After both are melted immerse the dipper and allow it to acquire the temperature of the melted lead. Then fill the dipper and, with the nozzle horizontal, raise it two or three inches above the surface of the lead in the pot. With the mould in the other hand, turn it sidewise and bring the pouring hole of the mould to the nozzle of the dipper. Then, with the mould and dipper in contact, tilt or turn both in this position until the dipper is over the mould and the nozzle vertical as shown.

IG. 87.—MOULDING BULLETS.

The weight or pressure of the lead in the dipper is thus utilized to force the lead into and completely fill the corners of the mould. It will be necessary to mould forty or fifty bullets before the mould acquires the proper temperature and casts first-class bullets. All imperfect bullets should be thrown back into the melting-pot. Experience has shown that the best results are obtained when the lead and mould are at such temperature that two or three seconds elapse before the lead solidifies in the pouring hole after the nozzle has been removed from it. Do not allow the lead to get red-hot, as it oxidizes very rapidly and more dross forms on its surface at that temperature. The dross should be skimmed off frequently and not allowed to collect in the dipper. A new mould will not cast perfect bullets until the surfaces in contact with the lead are free from oil and have become oxidized, assuming a deep blue colour.

Provide a soft surface for the bullets to fall upon after releasing them from the mould, as they are easily deformed while hot. The sliding top or "cut-off" should be operated by pressing down the lever end on a board or table, or striking the lever with a small wooden mallet. The mould is then opened, and the bullet drops out. If the bullet sticks in the mould, strike the empty half of the mould on the outside, directing the blow toward the bullet. This will jar the bullet out of the mould without difficulty.

Never strike the mould with a hammer or any hard substance, and never attempt to pry a bullet out of the mould or touch the interior surface with an iron implement, tool, or anything that will mar it. The least indentation of the sharp edges of the mould will cause the bullets to stick and make them imperfect. After using the mould, oil the exterior and the surfaces of the joint while warm, wrap in a dry cloth, and keep in a dry place where it will not rust. It is a good plan to leave the last bullet (with the neck cut off) in the mould until used again.

The fit of the bullets is very important. Nearly all the bullets for revolver cartridges were originally designed to be used with black powder. Many of them were slightly under size and have concave bases which upset sufficiently, on the ignition of the regulation powder charge, to fill the grooves of the barrel. Reduced charges of black powder, and smokeless powders, even in full charges, seldom upset the bases of these bullets, and the powder gas escapes around the sides of the bullet, which is known as "gas cutting." This is fatal to accuracy. For smokeless powders and reduced loads the concave cavity at the base of the bullet must be large enough to reduce the thickness of the outer rim of the bullet and weaken it so it will be expanded sufficiently by the powder to fill the grooves of the barrel; or the diameter of the bullet should be increased so as to produce the same effect.

A simple test to determine the fit of the bullet is to force it into a clean barrel, and then hold the barrel in the direction of a window or bright light. If light can be seen in any of the grooves around the bullet, it is too small for smokeless powder. The remedy is to have the bullet mould reamed out and enlarged so the bullets will be the proper size.

To determine the actual diameter of the bore of a pistol or revolver, oil the inside of the barrel liberally and then force a bullet into it a couple of inches. With a short wooden cleaning rod, hold the bullet in that position while you drive against it with another rod from the opposite direction, swaging it so as to fill the barrel. This must be done gently and carefully so as not to strain or injure the barrel. The bullet is then driven out and carefully measured with a micrometer gauge.

Many who mould their own bullets prefer to order the mould to cast the bullets the exact size to fit the barrel; while others prefer to have the mould cast the bullet one or two thousandths of an inch too large, and then pass them through a sizing tool, reducing them to the correct size. The latter method insures absolute uniformity.

For smokeless powders the bullets are generally cast a little harder than for black powder, the proportions being from 30 to 1, to 20 to 1, of lead and tin, respectively. To secure good results, the bullets should not vary more than 1/200 in weight.

The next operation after moulding the bullets is to lubricate them. A good lubricant may be prepared by melting together 1½ lbs. of Japan wax, 1 lb. of mutton tallow, and 1 lb. of Vaseline. The bullets should be set in a shallow pan, bases down, and with a small space separating them. The lubricant can then be poured around them until it rises high enough to fill the top cannelure. After cooling, the bullets are cut out of the lubricant by forcing them into the mouth of a specially prepared shell with the top or head cut off. Each bullet is picked up in this way and then pushed out with a round rod. Any lubricant on the base of the bullet should be removed with a cloth before loading. An excellent machine for lubricating bullets is made by the Ideal Manufacturing Company. The machine sizes and lubricates the bullet at one operation. It is rapid, clean, and performs the work perfectly.

Powders.—American powder manufacturers have no uniform practice in regard to designating the different grades of powder, sizes of grains, etc. The powders that give the best results under certain conditions must therefore be classified. The following black powders are best suited for ammunition in which the charge is ten to twenty grains:

American Powder Mills Rifle Cartridge No. 4.

Hazard Powder Company's "Kentucky Rifle F F G."

E. I. Dupont de Nemours & Company's "Dupont Rifle F F G."

Laflin & Rand Powder Company's "Orange Rifle Extra F F G."

King Powder Company's "Semi-smokeless F F G."

When the charge is less than ten grains in weight, one size finer grain of the above powders should be used; and for charges heavier than twenty grains, one size coarser grain will give the best results.

Lesmok powder, now so extensively used for .22-calibre rim fire ammunition, is a combination of black powder with high-grade guncotton.

For reduced or gallery charges, the high-grade quick-burning shotgun powders are sometimes used, such as "Hazard's Electric," "Dupont's Diamond Grain," etc. These powders should not be used in full charges, and if compressed in the shell will give very irregular shooting.

Smokeless powder differs from black not only in composition but also in the phenomena that attend combustion. Special conditions are therefore created which have an important bearing on the results. Smokeless powders are divided into two general classes, designated as "bulk" and "dense,"the former having approximately the same strength as an equal bulk of black powder, while the same quantity by bulk of the latter may have from five to ten times the strength of black powder.

The bulk powders may be used very much the same as black powder, except that they should never be compressed. No air space is required between the powder and the bullet. Dupont's Smokeless Rifle Powder No. 2 and Hazard's Smokeless Rifle Powder No. 2 are good examples of the bulk powders. Dupont's R. S. Q. is a bulk powder that has recently been introduced. It gives fair results in pistol and revolver ammunition in full charges, but is not as well adapted for reduced or gallery loads. It requires an air space for the best results.

The dense powders, such as Bullseye, Du Pont Pistol No. 3, Walsrode, and others, on account of their concentrated form, must be manipulated with great care and precision. The same quantity by bulk as black powder of any of these would in many cases cause disaster. Special shells with an annular crease, which only admits the bullet a certain distance into the mouth of the shell, and providing an air space, should in all cases be used with these powders.

Nearly all varieties of smokeless powders require a certain amount of confinement in order to secure complete combustion, and do not give good results unless the shell is crimped securely to the bullet.

A table giving the proper charges is supplied by all the manufacturers of smokeless powders, suitable for revolver and pistol shooting. These charges should in no case be increased. If it is desired to adapt a smokeless charge to a special bullet, which gives good results with black powder, the approximate equivalent in smokeless powder can easily be calculated from the powder company's table of charges. If the calculated charge does not give good results, compare the penetration of the smokeless charge with the black powder charge, and modify the former until it gives approximately the same penetration as the latter. If this does not correct the difficulty, the fit of the bullet should be investigated, and possibly it may have to be increased in size slightly and hardened before the best results will be obtained.

No attempt should be made to secure higher velocities or greater penetration with the ordinary lead bullet than is obtained with black powder. Such results can only be produced with hard alloy or jacketed bullets, special rifling, etc., and in arms designed to withstand the severe conditions incident to such augmented effects. Excessive charges in regulation arms, besides being extremely dangerous, are likely to cause the bullet to strip the rifling and lead the barrel.

The most recent activity in the matter of smokeless powders is the series of experiments with the U. S. Government pyro-cellulose formula. The powders are cut to such dimensions as will fit them for both pistol and rifle cartridges. This powder has the advantage of causing much less erosion than the nitro-glycerine powders and for that reason will probably appeal to the ammunition manufacturers and consumers, to such an extent as to secure its adoption, if the experiments now in progress prove to be satisfactory from a ballistic standpoint.

Reloading.—Suitable tools for reloading are furnished by the Ideal Manufacturing Company, Smith & Wesson, and the Winchester Repeating Arms Company. These usually consist of one or more combination tools, with which the various operations may be performed with rapidity and precision.

In reloading ammunition the one thing to be borne in mind above all else is *uniformity*. No matter how excellent may be the quality of the powder, or how perfect the bullets, if there is any variation in quantity, size, etc., the results will surely be irregular and disappointing. The bullets should be of the same diameter and weight, the mouth of the shells of uniform size, the powder accurately measured, and all the details in the operation of loading each shell should be as nearly identical as it is possible to make them.

Shells that have been loaded with black powder will corrode very rapidly if not properly and promptly cared for. The primer should be extracted from the shells as soon as practicable after firing. The shells should then be immersed in hot soap-suds and stirred around briskly until thoroughly washed. If it is desired to brighten them or to remove corrosion, add one tablespoonful of sulphuric acid to each quart of suds. Rinse the shells in two clean boiling waters by agitating them as before, and then dry them by exposure to sunlight or mild heat. Intense heat will draw the temper of the shells and ruin them.

If the shells were originally crimped they will have to be opened with the tool so as to admit the bullet without shaving off or abrading its surface. The Ideal Manufacturing Company can furnish a special plug, screwed to the tool, by which the primer may be extracted and the mouth of the shell opened in one operation, the tool automatically releasing the shell from the plug, thus making the operation of opening the mouth of the shell rapid and easy. In the case of smokeless powders the cleaning of the shells is not so important, but is desirable, as some of the powders leave a sticky residue which interferes more or less with the reloading process.

After the shells have been cleaned and dried the new primers may be placed in position. In doing this be sure to seat them firmly on the bottom of the pocket and below the surface of the head of the shell. This will prevent misfires and premature explosions.

The measuring of the powder charge is the most important detail in reloading ammunition. There are several devices to measure powder that are convenient and fairly accurate. Those furnished by the Ideal Manufacturing Company, designated as No. 5 or No. 6, and those made by H. M. Pope are the best.[2]

The usual method is to measure the powder with a charge cup that is supplied with the reloading tools. A quantity of the powder should be poured from the can into a small box and the charge cup dipped into it and filled. With a thin lead-pencil tap the cup lightly two or three times on the side to settle the powder uniformly. If the powder settles below the top of the cup dip the cup into the powder again and fill it, being careful not to tilt the cup so as to disturb the powder already in it. Strike off the powder in the cup with the pencil and pour it into the shell. By measuring the powder in this way and verifying it by weighing each charge in a delicate balance, a high degree of skill may be acquired in a short time. Ordinary revolver charges should not vary more than one-tenth of a grain in weight.

The charge cup method is preferred by many in measuring smokeless powders, as some varieties, being coarse grained and light in weight, are liable to form large voids. Such voids are invariably corrected when the charge cup is tapped and the powder settles.

2. See Gunsmithing, Repairs, etc., in the Appendix.

After the desired quantity of shells has been primed and charged with powder, the bullets, properly lubricated, are started into the shells by hand and then one by one the cartridges are placed in the reloading tool, which seats the bullet and crimps the shell.

In reduced black powder charges, when the bullet is seated below the mouth of the shell, the tool should be adjusted so as not to crimp the shell.

In loading cartridges in which the shells are not crimped on the bullets, it is very important that both the shells and the bullets should be absolutely uniform in size, so that the fit, and consequently the friction, of the bullets in the shell will be the same in all cases. By reloading some of the shells oftener than others or with different charges, the expansion of the shells will vary and the bullets will fit more or less tightly. Such ammunition when fired will vary in elevation. It is well to begin with new shells using the same load in them and reloading them the same number of times. Even with the same charge and under apparently identical conditions a few of the shells will expand differently. This variation will, however, be readily discovered in seating the bullets with the tool. Cartridges in which the bullets seat with greater or less effort than the average should be carefully separated from the rest and not used when fine shooting is required.

In reloading ammunition with spherical or "round" bullets the neck of the bullet should be up, opposite the powder side. In this position the neck is always in sight, and any turning of the bullet so as to bring the neck on the side and in contact with the barrel will be apparent and can be corrected. All round bullets should be at least 1/1000 of an inch larger in diameter than the bottom of the grooves of the barrel. This causes them to deform slightly on the circle of contact with the barrel, and creates a narrow cylindrical surface around the bullet, securing a better bearing and greatly increasing the accuracy. It also insures the tight fitting of the bullet in the shell, preventing it from being displaced by the recoil. If round bullets fit loosely, or if there is the slightest imperfection in the bullet where it comes in contact with the shell or the barrel, "gas-cutting" will result and hot lubricant is liable to pass by the bullet into the powder charge. In either case the accuracy is impaired.

When round bullets are used, the lubricant must be applied after they have been seated. This can best be done with a small brush. The brush is dipped into melted lubricant and then passed around the bullet where it is in contact with the shell. Too much lubricant is undesirable. At least three-quarters of the surface of[Pg 165] the bullet should project above the lubricant. By keeping the lubricant at a constant temperature, the quantity adhering to the brush will be approximately the same and the results uniform.

In reduced loads, when black powder or "bulk" smokeless powder is used, the bullets may be seated so as to just touch the powder charge; never so as to compress it. When "dense" smokeless powder is used, a suitable air space must always be provided. This is necessary both when round or conical bullets are used.

With all forms of conical bullets and when using either "dense" or "bulk" smokeless powder, in full or reduced charges, better results are invariably obtained by seating the bullets in the regulation position and crimping the shells moderately and uniformly on the middle of the front band of the bullet.

Ammunition for automatic pistols may also be reloaded by hand, but there is much less economy than in reloading other ammunition. When the full charge is used, a metal-cased bullet is required which must be purchased from the manufacturers. Reduced loads with lead bullets will operate in some of the pistols only. An overcharge of powder for a lead bullet will lead the barrel and is liable to cause difficulty with the mechanism, and accidents. Only experienced persons familiar with the operations of loading the rimless shells and whether or not the arms will operate with the charges they propose to use, should attempt reloading this ammunition.

The United States Revolver Association

This Association was founded on March 5, 1900, and incorporated in January, 1904. It is the recognized national organization of the revolver and pistol marksmen of the United States of America.

Its objects are: to foster and develop revolver and pistol shooting; to establish and preserve records; to classify arms; and to encourage and conduct friendly matches between members and clubs in this country, as well as with the marksmen of other countries.

The officers of the Association, excepting the secretary, serve without pay. There is no initiation fee. The annual dues are only $1.00. The membership, scattered from Maine to the Philippines, Alaska to the Canal Zone, includes all the well-known shots of the country.

The Association has conducted five international revolver matches, all of which were won by the United States. It selects the members of and is responsible for the United States teams in the Olympic and all other international matches. It has established the Annual Outdoor and Indoor Championship Matches, the U. S. R. A. Indoor League and provided suitable trophies and medals. It has formulated uniform rules and regulations governing pistol and revolver shooting. In the record books of the Association are inscribed and preserved all the scores in the Annual Championship Contests, the individual and team league series, the scores of contestants, shooting for rating medals and the "best on record" performances, together with details concerning the arms and ammunition used. The Association also publishes the *U. S. R. A. Bulletin*, a monthly devoted to all subjects of interest to the members, the subscription for which is included in the annual dues.

The Association is financially self-supporting. It has an increasing surplus in the treasury, which is devoted to the purchase of new trophies for additional matches.

All who are interested in pistol and revolver shooting, and who are in sympathy with the aims and purposes of the Association, are cordially invited to join it. Forms of application for membership and other information will be supplied by the Secretary-Treasurer on request.

The officers of the Association for 1915 are as follows:

President: Col. W. H. Whigam, Chicago, Ill.

1st Vice-President: Capt. R. H. Sayre, New York, N.Y.

2nd Vice-President: C. C. Crossman, St. Louis, Mo.

3rd Vice-President: C. W. Linder, San Francisco, Cal.

4th Vice-President: Dr. R. J. Mullikin, Baltimore, Md.

5th Vice-President: Dr. H. E. Sears, Boston, Mass.

Secretary-Treasurer: J. B. Crabtree, Yalesville, Conn.

CONSTITUTION
Article 1—*Name*
The name of this organization shall be the United States Revolver Association.
Article 2—*Object*
The object of this association shall be the encouragement of revolver and pistol shooting.
Article 3—*Membership*
The membership shall consist of three classes: Members, Honorary Members, Associate Members.

Any reputable citizen of the United States is eligible for membership.

Any reputable person interested in revolver and pistol shooting is eligible for Honorary or Associate membership.

Members and Associate members may be admitted by vote of the executive committee and by paying the regular dues. Honorary members may be elected at a regular meeting of the association and shall be exempt from dues.

Honorary and Associate members shall be entitled to all the privileges of the association, except the right to vote.

[See Art. 7 for Life membership.]
Article 4—*Officers*

The officers of this association shall be a president, five vice-presidents and a secretary-treasurer, who shall constitute the executive committee. They shall be elected by a majority vote by ballot at the annual meeting of the association, and hold office for one year or until their successors are elected.

Article 5—*Duties of Officers*

The president shall preside at all meetings of the association and may call meetings of the association at any time, one week's notice by mail being given of such meeting by the secretary-treasurer. The approval of the president shall be necessary on all bills before they are paid. The vice-presidents in the order of their seniority shall perform the duties of the president in his absence and shall have responsible charge, subject to the executive committee, of the affairs of the association in their respective localities. The secretary-treasurer shall keep the minutes of all meetings and take charge of the correspondence of the association. He shall receive all dues and pay all bills approved by the president, and keep account of all the funds of the association. The executive committee shall have charge of the affairs of the association, shall elect members, appoint State governors to act as local representatives of the association, and shall have power to accept, decline, or issue challenges by a majority vote. Any member of the executive committee unable to be present at any meeting may vote by mail.

Article 6—*Vacancies in Office*

In case a vacancy should occur in any office, the remaining members of the executive committee shall have power to fill the vacancy until the next annual meeting.

Article 7—*Dues*

Section 1. The annual dues shall be one dollar, and shall be payable on election to membership and thereafter on the 1st of January in every year.

Section 2. Members in arrears for dues for a period of more than two years shall be suspended, but may reinstate themselves in full standing by paying their arrears in dues. Members may not resign from the association when in arrears for dues.

Section 3. The secretary-treasurer shall notify each member in arrears before placing his name on the suspended list.

Section 4. Any member of this association in good standing

may become a Life Member by vote of the executive committee and by paying into the treasury $25, such funds to be used by the association for the purchase of trophies.

Article 8—*Annual Meeting*

There shall be an annual meeting on the third Monday of January in each year, at which meeting the election of officers and members of the executive committee shall take place. Members not able to attend this meeting may send their ballots by mail to the secretary-treasurer, who shall deposit each ballot in the name of the absent member, and they shall be counted as if the member were present. Only members not in arrears for dues shall be entitled to vote. If there should be more than two candidates for any office, the candidate receiving the least number of votes shall be retired at each ballot until an election results. In case of a tie the presiding officer shall have the deciding vote.

Article 9—*Quorum*

Ten members shall constitute a quorum for the transaction of business.

ANNUAL CHAMPIONSHIP MATCHES

Outdoor Matches

Match A—Revolver Championship.—Open to everybody; distance, 50 yards; 50 shots in strings of ten shots on five Standard American targets, 8-inch bullseye, 10-ring 3.36 inches; arm, any revolver within the rules; ammunition, any; the score must be completed in one hour or less from the time of firing the first shot; entrance fee, $5; to members not in arrears for dues, $3; no re-entries.

National Prizes: *First*, the championship silver cup (value, $200), to be held by the winner until the next annual competition; inscribed on the cup, in raised ornamental letters, is, "This Cup Represents the Revolver Championship of the United States of America"; the name of the winner, the year and the score are also engraved on the cup each year; to the winner is also awarded a gold medal (value, $25), with the same inscription on the reverse side as appears on the cup.

Second, a gold and silver medal, with inscription on the reverse side.

Third, a silver medal, with inscription on the reverse side.

Fourth, a silver and bronze medal, with inscription on the reverse side.

Fifth, a bronze medal, with inscription on the reverse side.

A bronze honour medal of the same design is also awarded to every competitor, not a prize winner, making a score of 425 or better.

State Prizes.—For more than three entries in any State the association awards three prizes emblematic of State honours: *First prize*, a silver and gold medal; *second prize*, a silver medal; *third prize*, a bronze medal. For three entries, only the first two prizes are awarded.

Winners and Scores

1900	A. L. Himmelwright	422
1901	John A. Dietz	419
1902	Thomas Anderton	438
1903	J. E. Gorman	454
1904	Dr. I. R. Calkins	451
1905	John A. Dietz	455
1906	John A. Dietz	444
1907	John A. Dietz	445
1908	R. H. Sayre	462
1909	Dr. I. R. Calkins	455
1910	Dr. John R. Hicks	458
1911	George Armstrong	467
1912	A. M. Poindexter	467
1913	A. P. Lane	467
1914	A. P. Lane	458

Match B—Pistol Championship.—Open to everybody; distance, 50 yards; 50 shots on five targets as in Match A; arm, any pistol within the rules; ammunition, any; the score must be completed in one hour or less from the time of firing the first shot; entrance fee, $5; to members not in arrears for dues, $3; no re-entries.

National Prizes: *First*, the championship silver cup (value, $175), to be held by the winner until the next annual competition; inscribed on the cup, in raised ornamental letters, is, "This Cup Represents the Pistol Championship of the United States of America"; the name of the winner, the year and the score are also engraved on the cup each year; to the winner is also awarded a gold medal (value, $25), with the same inscription on the reverse side as appears on the cup.

Second, a silver and gold medal, with inscription on the reverse side.

Third, a silver medal, with inscription on the reverse side.

Fourth, a bronze and silver medal, with inscription on the reverse side.

Fifth, a bronze medal, with inscription on the reverse side.

A bronze honour medal of the same design is also awarded to every competitor, not a prize winner, making a score of 435 or better.

State Prizes.—The same as in Match A.

Winners and Scores

Year	Name	Score
1900	J. B. Crabtree	427
1901	Thomas Anderton	453
1902	Thomas Anderton	463
1903	Thomas Anderton	457
1904	E. H. Kessler	464
1905	John A. Dietz	465
1906	John A. Dietz	448
1907	P. Hanford	455
1908	J. E. Gorman	468
1909	Dr. I. R. Calkins	464
1910	John A. Dietz	462
1911	Parmly Hanford	466
1912	L. P. Castaldini	461
1913	Dr. I. R. Calkins	469
1914	George Armstrong	476

Match C—Military Championship.—Open to everybody; distance, 50 yards; 75 shots in strings of five shots on fifteen targets as in Match A; each string must be shot within the time limit of 15 seconds, taking time from the command, Fire; misfires and shots lost on account of the arm becoming disabled while firing any string will be scored zero; if a shot is fired after the time limit has elapsed, the shot of highest count will be deducted from the score; no cleaning allowed; arm, any military revolver, or any military magazine pistol within the rules; ammunition, the full charge service cartridge, or equivalent factory loaded ammunition approved by the executive committee, brought to the firing point in unbroken packages; the score must be completed on the same day; no sighting shots will be allowed after beginning the score; entrance fee, $5; to members not in arrears for dues, $3; no re-entries.

National Prizes: *First*, the championship silver trophy (an elaborate silver bowl, value $450), to be held by the winner until the next annual competition; the trophy bears the inscription, "The Military Revolver Championship of the United States of America"; the name of the winner, the year, and the score are also engraved on the trophy each year; to the winner is also awarded a gold medal (value, $25), with the same inscription on the reverse side as appears on the trophy.

Second, a silver and gold medal, with inscription on the reverse side.

Third, a silver medal, with inscription on the reverse side.

Fourth, a bronze and silver medal, with inscription on the reverse side.

Fifth, a bronze medal, with inscription on the reverse side.

A bronze honour medal of the same design is also awarded to every competitor, not a prize winner, making a score of 500 or better.

State Prizes.—The same as in Match A.

Winners and Scores

Year	Winner	Score
1900	R. H. Sayre	300 [1]
1901	R. H. Sayre	325 [1]
1902	R. H. Sayre	579
1903	R. H. Sayre	565
1904	Thomas Anderton	585
1905	Thos. LeBoutillier	504
1906	R. H. Sayre	583
1907	R. H. Sayre	536
1908	C. F. G. Armstrong	568
1909	Col. W. H. Whigam	580
1910	Col. W. H. Whigam	591
1911	A. P. Lane	605
1912	Dr. J. H. Snook	621
1913	Dr. J. H. Snook	625
1914	C. M. McCutchen	627

Match D—Military Record Match.—Open to everybody; distance, 50 yards; five consecutive strings of five shots under the same conditions as Match C; entrance fee, $2; to members not in arrears for dues, $1; entries unlimited.

National Prizes: *First*, a gold trophy, a laurel wreath surrounding a scroll, mounted on an ebony shield; (value, $150); between the scroll and the wreath is a ribbon on which, in raised letters, is, "The United

---

1. In 1900 and 1901 the military target with a 4x5-inch elliptical bullseye was used. The bullseye counted 5 and the possible was 375. Since then the Standard American target with the 8-inch bullseye has been used. Prior to 1904 twenty-five shots were fired at each of three ranges—25, 50, and 75 yards. That year the other ranges were discontinued and the 75 shots have since been fired at 50 yards only.

States Revolver Association"; at the top of the scroll is engraved, "Military Record Match." The name of the winner, the year, and the score for each year are engraved on the scroll below; this trophy is held by the winner until the next annual competition, and is to become the property of the competitor winning it three times.

Second, a silver medal, with inscription on the reverse side.

Third, a bronze medal, with inscription on the reverse side.

A bronze honor medal of the same design is also awarded to every competitor, not a prize winner, making a score of 175 or better.

This match was instituted in 1902. Being a re-entry match, it affords good practice under the same conditions as Match C.

No State prizes are awarded in this match.

Winners and Scores	
1902 Thomas Anderton	206
1903 Thomas Anderton	202
1904 Thomas Anderton	206
1905 Thos. LeBoutillier	178
1906 Thos. LeBoutillier	192
1907 Thos. LeBoutillier	191
1908 C. F. G. Armstrong	194
1909 C. F. G. Armstrong	204
1910 Samuel Peterson	215
1911 A. P. Lane	208
1912 Dr. J. H. Snook	212
1913 C. M. McCutchen	217
1914 Dr. J. H. Snook	221

Match E—Military Revolver Team Match.—Open to one team of four men from any regularly organized Rifle or Revolver Club, the police force of any city, or any Regiment, Battalion, or separate organization from any of the organized Military or Naval forces of any civilized country.

Distance, 50 yards; five consecutive strings of 5 shots each under the same conditions as Match C; arm, any military revolver or magazine pistol within the rules; ammunition, full charge factory loaded, brought to the firing point in unbroken packages; entrance fee, $15; to affiliated clubs, $10; no re-entries.

Prizes: *First*, the Winans Trophy (a "Broncho Buster" in bronze, mounted on an elaborate red porphyry marble base; value, $500). The name of the winning club or organization, the year and the score, will be engraved on the base. The trophy to be held by the winning organization until the next annual competition. A silver and gold medal will also be awarded to each member of the winning team, with inscription on the reverse side.

Second, a silver medal to each member of the team, with inscription on the reverse side.

Third, a bronze and silver medal to each member of the team, with an inscription on the reverse side.

Fourth, a bronze medal to each member of the team, with an inscription on the reverse side.

This match was instituted in October, 1908, when Mr. Walter Winans (Life member) presented the association with an appropriate trophy.

Winners and Scores

1909	Squadron "A," N. G. N.Y.	698
1910	1st Cavalry Ill. N. G	708
1911	1st Cavalry Ill. N. G.	725
1913	Denver Rev. Club	776
1914	Denver Rev. Club	799

Match F—Pocket Revolver Championship.—Open to everybody; 25 shots at 50 yards in strings of 5 shots on five targets, as in Match A; each string to be fired within 30 seconds after the command, "Fire." Arm, any pocket revolver of .32 or larger calibre or any pocket magazine pistol of .25 to .38 calibre inclusive, weighing less than 1¾ pounds within the rules; cleaning not allowed; ammunition, the same as Match C. Entrance fee, $4; to members not in arrears for dues, $2; no re-entries.

National Prizes: *First*, a gold medal, with inscription on the reverse side.

Second, a silver and gold medal, with inscription on the reverse side.

Third, a silver medal, with inscription on the reverse side.

Fourth, a bronze and silver medal, with inscription on the reverse side.

Fifth, a bronze medal, with inscription on the reverse side.

A bronze honour medal will also be awarded to any competitor not a prize winner making a score of 175 or better.

State Prizes.—For five or more entries the following prizes will be awarded: 1st prize, a gold and silver medal; 2nd prize, a silver medal;

3rd prize, a bronze medal.

Winners and Scores

1909	C. W. Klett	203
1910	C. E. Orr	202
1911	A. P. Lane	211
1912	Dr. O. A. Burgson	208
1913	Col. W. H. Whigam	210
1914	Dr. J. H. Snook	214

GRAND AGGREGATE MEDALS

In addition to the regular matches the association awards Grand Aggregate Medals to the contestants making the highest aggregate scores in Championship Matches A, B, C, and F.

The following new matches have been added to the annual contests of the U. S. R. A.:

Match G—Novice Limited Re-Entry Match.—Outdoor Event.—Open to all amateurs who have never won an important prize in our branch of sport.

Winners of honours in our National Championships, first and second place honours in our State Championships, National honours in this match, professional shooters and those who have won place in important matches other than those of the U. S. R. A. are barred.

Score: Twenty-five shots in five strings of five shots each.

Time: Thirty minutes.

Weapon and Ammunition: Any allowed in Matches A and B.

Prizes: National—As in Match A.

State: As in Match F.

An honour medal will be given for a score of 210 or better that wins no other prize.

Entrance Fee: First entry $2. There may be four re-entries at $1.00 each. As yet we have a silver cup for only the Indoor Match.

Match H—Revolver Handicap.—Indoor and Outdoor Event.—Arm, any revolver within the rules for Match A. Ammunition any. Twenty-five shots in strings of five shots each. Time, thirty minutes per score. Entrance fee, $3 to paid-up members, $5 to all other persons.

The possible, 250, will be taken as a basis and a contestant allowed a handicap thought likely to be necessary to make his score in this match equal the possible. The fifty-shot and twenty-five shot revolver records of the contestants on file with the secretary will be taken as the basis of handicapping. The fifty shot records will be reduced to twenty-five shot equivalents.

Prizes: National medals as in Match A. If the whole number of contestants in this match exceeds twenty, then state medals will also be awarded as in Match A.

A bronze honour medal will be awarded for the highest score less handicap if it wins no other prize.

Winners and Scores

Indoor	Handicap	Outdoor	Handicap
1915—F. J. Dreher	25	I. B. Humphrey	45.5
1916—F. L. Simmonds	47.5		

Match I—Pistol Handicap.—Indoor and Outdoor Event.—Arm, Colt .22 automatic and any pistol allowed in Match B. Ammunition, any. Entrance fee, $3 to paid-up members, $5 to all other persons. Twenty-five shots in strings of five shots each. Time of score, thirty minutes.

Prizes as in Match H.

Each entrant may name his own handicap. It must be claimed and mailed in a letter bearing a post mark prior to the shooting of the match.

Scores with handicaps exceeding the possible will be penalized three points for each point of excess.

Winners and Scores

Indoor	Handicap	Outdoor	Handicap
1915—Rich'd Henderson	75	J. H. Snook	16
1916—Stanley Runck	30		

Match J—Police Team Match.—Indoor Only.—Limited to members of a uniformed police force who must furnish credentials to the effect that they have been enrolled one year or more. Five men teams.

Arm, any revolver with a barrel not more than 4½ inches long, trigger pull not less than three pounds, calibre not less than .32. Twenty shots per man. Five-shot strings. Time two minutes per string. Time to be entered on target and signed by timer. Ammunition, the full factory charge for the most powerful cartridge the arm will chamber. Entrance fee, $10 per team.

Prizes: Medals for the members of the first three teams. Gold and silver; silver; bronze. Six or more entries required to fill the match. Entry fees refunded if "No contest." With ten or more teams entering, silver medals emblematic of state championship honour will be awarded for three contesting teams from one state. With four or more teams from one state, silver medals will be given the first team, bronze medals the second. National medals take precedence.

Ties will be decided by the fewest shots of low count.

Winners and Scores
1915—Portland. Ore

R. H. Craddock	162
J. H. Young	157
W. D. Humphrey	155
J. T. Moore	46
	776

1916—San Francisco, Calif.

S. Carr	165
W. R. Proll	157
J. M. Mann	157
T. J. Sullivan	143
E. C. Lange	140
	762

First, a gold medal, with inscription on the reverse side.
Second, a silver medal, with inscription on the reverse side.
Third, a bronze medal, with inscription on the reverse side.

The grand aggregate will be computed by adding the total scores of the Matches A, B, and F, and one-fifth of the total score in Match C.

The grand aggregate medals are considered the highest honours in the gift of the association.

Winners and Scores

1909 C. Dominic	1187.8
1910 A. P. Lane	1215.8
1911 A. P. Lane	1236
1912 Parmly Hanford	1228
1913 A. P. Lane	1261
1914 A. P. Lane	1242

Revolver Championship.—Open to everybody; distance, 20 yards; light must be artificial; 50 shots on ten Standard American targets, bullseye 2.72 inches and 10-ring 1.12 inches in diameter, respectively; arm, any revolver within the rules; ammunition, any. The score must be completed in one hour or less from the time of firing the first shot. Entrance fee, $5; to members not in arrears for dues, $3; no re-entries.

National Prizes: *First*, a silver cup (value, $40), bearing the names and scores of the winners, to be held until the next annual competition, the cup to become the property of the person winning it three times.

Second, a gold and silver medal, with inscription on the reverse side.

Third, a silver medal, with inscription on the reverse side.

Fourth, a silver and bronze medal, with inscription on the reverse side.

Fifth, a bronze medal, with inscription on the reverse side.

A bronze honour medal will also be awarded to any competitor, not a prize winner, making a score of 425 or better.

State Prizes.—The same as in Match A of the Outdoor Matches.

Winners and Scores

1901	W. E. Petty	439
1902	W. E. Petty	439
1903	W. H. Luckett	437
1904	Sidney E. Sears	478
1905	Sidney E. Sears	461
1906	Sidney E. Sears	451
1907	Wm. G. Krieg	454
1908	R. H. Sayre	454
1909	R. H. Sayre	455
1910	Oscar I. Olson	461
1911	C. C. Crossman	455
1912	Dr. J. R. Hicks	457
1913	P. J. Dolfin	469
1914	Dr. W. E. Quicksall	457

Pistol Championship.—Open to everybody; distance, 20 yards; light must be artificial; 50 shots on ten Standard American targets; bullseye 2.72 inches and 10-ring 1.12 inches in diameter, respectively;

arm, any pistol within the rules; ammunition, any. The score must be completed in one hour or less from the time of firing the first shot. Entrance fee, $5; to members not in arrears for dues, $3; no re-entries.

National and State Prizes: The same as in the indoor Revolver Championship, except that honor medals are awarded for scores of 435 or better.

Winners and Scores

1901	R. H. Sayre	433
1902	R. H. Sayre	448
1903	Thomas Anderton	460
1904	E. H. Kessler	450
1905	R. H. Sayre	451
1906	John A. Dietz	447
1907	John A. Dietz	455
1908	R. P. Prentys	455
1909	Frank Fromm	456
1910	R. H. Sayre	454
1911	George Armstrong	473
1912	A. P. Lane	469
1913	Dr. C. H. Wilson	465
1914	Dr. J. H. Snook	468

Pocket Revolver Championship.—Open to everybody; 25 shots at 20 yards in strings of five shots on five Standard American targets; each string to be fired within 30 seconds after the command, "Fire." Arm, any pocket revolver of .32 calibre or larger, within the rules.

Magazine pistols not allowed. Ammunition, full charge, factory loaded, brought to the firing point in unbroken packages. Entrance fee, $4; to members not in arrears for dues, $2.

Prizes.—The same as in Match F of the Outdoor Matches.

Winners and Scores

1909	Wm. G. Krieg	190
1910	Dr. M. R. Moore	202
1911	Col. W. H. Whigam	195
1912	John A. Dietz	205
1913	Hans Roedder	206
1914	Dr. J. H. Snook	213

Match G Novice Limited Re-Entry Match.—Open to all amateurs who have never won an important prize in pistol or revolver contests. (Winners of prizes in National contests and first and second prizes in State contests, all expert shots, etc., are barred.) Twenty-five shots at 20 yards in five strings on five Standard American targets. Time, 30 minutes to complete the score after firing the first shot. Arm, any revolver or any pistol within the rules. Ammunition, any. Entrance fee, first entry, $3; to members not in arrears for dues, $2. There may be four re-entries at $1 each, but the score for the last re-entry only to count.

National and State Prizes:—The same as in Match F of the Outdoor Matches.

Winners and Scores
1913 R. S. Everett   231
1914 Robert Mills   229

RULES AND REGULATIONS GOVERNING THE CHAMPIONSHIP MATCHES OF THE U. S. R. A.

1. *General Conditions.*—Competitors must make themselves acquainted with the rules and regulations of the association, as the plea of ignorance will receive no consideration. The rulings and decisions of the executive committee are final in all cases. These rules are for general application, but will not apply in cases where the special conditions of any match conflict with them.

2. *Classification of Arms.*—

(a) Any revolver. A revolver of any calibre. Maximum length of barrel, including cylinder, 10 inches. Minimum trigger pull, 2½ pounds. Sights may be adjustable but they must be strictly open, in front of the hammer and not over 10 inches apart.

(b) Any pistol. A pistol of any calibre. Maximum length of barrel, 10 inches. Minimum trigger pull, 2 pounds. Sights may be adjustable but they must be strictly open, in front of the hammer and not over 10 inches apart.

(c) Military revolver or pistol. A revolver, or a magazine pistol, that has been adopted by any civilized government for the armament of its army or navy. Maximum weight, 2¾ pounds. Maximum length of barrel, 7½ inches. Minimum trigger pull, 4 pounds. Fixed open sights. Rear sights of magazine pistols may be adjustable for elevation only.

(d) Pocket revolver. A revolver having a maximum weight of 2 pounds. Maximum length of barrel, 4 inches; Minimum trigger pull, 4 pounds. Sights and model must be such as not to hinder quick drawing of the weapon from the pocket or holster.

3. *Loading, Firing, Timing, and Cleaning.*—In all revolver and pistol matches the weapon must not be loaded until the competitor has taken his position at the firing point. The barrel must always be kept vertical or pointed towards the target. After the target is in position and a match or record score has been begun, in case of an accidental discharge or of defective ammunition, if the bullet comes out of the barrel it will be scored a shot. The timing in matches C, D, E, and F will be as follows: The competitor standing at the firing point with the arm loaded, not cocked, and the barrel pointing in a direction not less than 45 degrees from the target, will signify to the scorer when he is ready to begin each string.

The scorer, stop watch in hand, will then give the command, "Fire," *after which* the competitor may cock and aim his weapon and shoot his string. At the expiration of the time limit the scorer will announce "Time." Misfires will be scored zero, only in Matches C, D, E, and F. Competitors may clean weapons in Matches A and B, and in the corresponding Indoor Championships, but no time allowance will be given for time spent in this way. All competitors will be required to finish their scores within the time limits specified, except in cases of accident, when the time may be extended at the discretion of the executive committee. Blowing through the barrel, to moisten it, will be considered cleaning.

In revolver matches the arm must not be used as a single loader or loaded so as to use a limited number of chambers in the cylinder. The cylinder must be charged with the full number of rounds for which it is chambered, and these must be shot consecutively. If scores are shot in ten shot strings, the cylinder shall be charged first with six rounds and then with four rounds. If the cylinder only contains five chambers, then the ten-shot strings may be shot in two strings of five each. In Matches C, D, E, and F and indoor or gallery events, the arm shall in all cases be charged with five rounds.

4. *Position.*—The position shall be standing, free from any support, the pistol or revolver being held in one hand, with arm extended, so as to be free from the body.

5. *Arms.*—Any revolver or pistol which in the opinion of the ex-

ecutive committee complies with the conditions specified in the various matches will be allowed to compete in those events. Revolvers or magazine pistols that have been adopted by any government for the armament of its army or navy, or such as in the opinion of the executive committee are suitable for military service, will be allowed in Matches C, D, and E. Among the arms which may be used in these matches are the .38-calibre Smith & Wesson or Colt Military; .44 Smith & Wesson, Military or Russian model; .38, .44 or .45 Colt New Service; .45 Smith & Wesson Scofield; .44 or .45 Colt, Single Action Army, Webley & Scott Mark IV, and the following magazine or automatic pistols: Colt, Webley & Scott, Luger, Borchardt, Mannlicher, Mauser, Mors.

6. *Sights.*—In open sights, the notch of the rear sight must be as wide on top as at any part. Aperture or peep sights or any covered or shaded sights will not be allowed. The use of a notch for the front sight will not be permitted. Sights may be smoked or blackened if desired. Sights on military arms, if modified to suit individuals, must remain strictly open, strong and substantial, and suitable for military use.

7. *Trigger-Pull.*—The trigger-pull as specified in the various events shall be determined by a test weight equal to the minimum pull applied at a point three-eighths of an inch from the end of the trigger and at right angles to the pin through the trigger.

8. *Ammunition.*—In Matches C, D, E, and F, and in the medal competition, where full charge ammunition is required, it may be the product of any reputable manufacturer. It must in all cases be brought to the firing point in unbroken boxes, with the label of the manufacturer intact.

9. *Targets.*—The 200-yard Standard American rifle target No. 1 (containing the 4-ring), with an 8-inch bullseye and showing in light lines the rings of the International Union target, shall be used in all matches at 50 yards. The scores will be counted on the Standard American target. The diameters of the rings of the Standard American target are as follows: 10-ring equals 3.36 inches; 9-ring equals 5.54 inches; 8-ring equals 8 inches; 7-ring equals 11 inches; 6-ring equals 14.8 inches; 5-ring equals 19.68 inches; 4-ring equals 26 inches; rest of target 28 inches by 28 inches counts 3. The same target reduced so that the bullseye or 8-ring is 2.72 inches in diameter and the 10-ring 1.12 inches in diameter, including the 4-ring 8.84 inches in diameter and the rest of the target 9½ inches by 9½ inches, counting 3, shall be

used for all matches at 20 yards.

10. *Marking and Scoring.*—In all matches new paper targets shall be furnished for each competitor. Not more than ten shots are to be fired on any target at 50 yards, and not more than five shots on any target in Matches C, D, E, and F, and for all shooting at 20 yards; the shot holes in all cases to remain uncovered and left as shot. Bullets touching, striking, or within a line on the target are to be scored the count of that line. The eye alone shall determine whether a bullet touches or not.

11. *Ties.*—Ties shall be decided as follows:

(1) By the score at the longest distance;

(2) by the score at the next longest distance;

(3) by the fewest number of shots of lowest count;

(4) by firing five shots each under the same conditions as the match and these rules in regard to ties, until decided.

12. *Supervision.*—The shooting in all the U. S. R. A. events must take place in the presence of at least two witnesses familiar with the rules, one of whom must be an authorized U. S. R. A. officer. This officer shall certify that each contestant has complied with all the U. S. R. A. regulations as to distance, weapon, time, ammunition, etc., noting same on the blank spaces provided on the score cards, and both witnesses shall sign the targets and said score cards in duplicate for each contestant.

13. *Protests.*—Any person who believes that an injustice has been done, or who dissents from the decision of any authorized executive officer of the association, may enter a protest on depositing $1 with said officer. Such protest must be in writing, in duplicate, and must be made within 24 hours after the incident on which it is based. One copy to be handed to the executive officer of the club or organization conducting the matches and the other copy to be mailed to the secretary-treasurer of the U. S. R. A. All protests will be investigated and passed upon by the executive committee, and, if sustained, the protest fee will be returned; otherwise it will be forfeited.

14. *Records.*—The shooting for records shall, when practicable, be done on the grounds or in a gallery of a regularly organized shooting association, military organization or club, and in the presence of at least two witnesses familiar with the U. S. R. A. rules, one of whom shall be an officer of the U. S. R. A. New targets of regulation size shall

be used. The foregoing rules and regulations and the conditions governing the championship matches of the U. S. R. A. must in all cases be observed and followed.

The record score shall begin with the first shot after the shooter has announced his intention to shoot for record; only the first ten shots will apply to the 10-shot record; the first twenty shots to the 20-shot record, and so on to 50 or 100 shots, as the shooter may elect. Such scores (multiples of 5 or 10 shots) for record must in all cases be completed within the same proportional time limit as is specified for the corresponding championship match; thus, in Match A, for example, the first 10 shots within 12 minutes, the first 20 shots within 24 minutes, etc. After finishing the record score, the targets shall be identified and signed by the witnesses as above designated.

The witnesses shall also prepare and sign a certificate of prescribed form, which, with the detailed score and all targets, shall be forwarded to the U. S. R. A., addressed to the secretary-treasurer. If all the conditions, rules and regulations have been complied with, the scoring correct, and if the score is higher than or equal to any previously made under the same conditions, it will be declared a new record. The score will then be entered as such in the record book of the association, and the shooter formally notified to that effect.

METHODS AND CUSTOMS TO BE FOLLOWED IN CONDUCTING THE
ANNUAL COMPETITIONS OF THE U. S. R. A.

The conditions under which local clubs may be authorized to conduct Championship Matches of the U. S. R. A. are as follows:

There must be not less than six members of the association residing within twenty-five miles of the proposed place of holding the contest and there must be not less than three entries in Championship Matches A, B, or C, or five entries in Match F. In matches offering National and State prizes the same entrance fee includes eligibility to both honours.

On the application of six or more members in good standing under the prescribed conditions, a U. S. R. A. official designated as the "governor" is appointed by the Association's executive committee and vested with the authority to supervise all Association shooting. The appointee is usually a member nominated by the local members. Besides supervising all the U. S. R. A. contests, the governor is the official representative of the Association in his locality, and has the custody of all supplies and the distribution of prizes, medals, etc. By this arrangement the U. S. R. A. members in all sections of the country obtain the same privileges and benefits and equal opportunity to enter the matches and competitions.

The U. S. R. A. will furnish numbered and certified targets and score cards, and will provide the prizes for the U. S. R. A. Championship and re-entry events; the club or organization to pay the expressage both ways on targets and all other supplies, to furnish the shooting facilities and conduct the contests free of expense to the association and turn over to the secretary-treasurer all the entrance fees for the U. S. R. A. events. This plan has in all cases given satisfactory results, because the practice shooting of the contestants in the local re-entry matches usually affords sufficient revenue to pay the expenses of the tournament.

When a competitor wishes to shoot in any of the events, he should exhibit his latest membership card (if a member) to the officers in charge, and after paying the entrance fee, a regular ticket or duplicate score card (furnished by the United States Revolver Association) is filled out and issued to him, which is his receipt for the entrance fee. His score need not necessarily be shot immediately after issuing the ticket. Competitors have the option of shooting in the order in which they pay for their entries. Tickets not used are forfeited: no entrance fees shall be refunded.

The requisite number of targets are issued when the competitor wishes to shoot his score. These must be numbered consecutively, they must have the competitor's name and the number of his score card written on them for identification, and must be shot in their numerical order.

The targets are usually tacked at the corners on alternating frames covered with canvas, over which heavy paper is pasted. Each target is left in position until the required number of shots have been fired at it, each shot being spotted and marked as fired [no pasters to be used]. When a string has been finished the target is lowered and the alternating target raised in position. After the score is completed the targets are brought to the firing point and delivered to the range officer.

When a competitor wishes to shoot his score, his arm must be inspected and passed by the officer in charge, who must see that it conforms with the rules and requirements of the event in which it is entered. Competitors who wish to enter in any of the events are urged to have their arms examined by the executive officer or committee in charge of the matches as soon as possible, so that in case there should be any exceptions made to the sights, the trigger-pull, or any other details, there will be an opportunity to have these exceptions corrected so as to comply with the requirements when the official test and inspection is made before shooting the score.

In Matches C, D, E, and F the scorer should have a reliable stop watch, so that the timing will be accurate. It is well, whenever possible, to have two men time the competitor, so as to have an additional check. A new target must be furnished for each string of five shots at each range. According to the rules, if a competitor starts to shoot a string of any score and his arm becomes disabled from any cause, those shots which reach the target within the time limit after the command, "Fire," will be counted as the complete score for the five shots. In the case of a disabled arm, the officer or committee in charge may allow the competitor to complete the remaining strings of his score with another arm. Shots on the paper target outside of the 4-ring count 3; shots missing the paper target count zero. After completing the score, when the duplicate score cards are filled out, the contestant takes the duplicate and the range officer retains the original record.

All unused targets and score cards are also to be forwarded to the secretary-treasurer, with a complete detailed account of entrance fees, supplies, etc.

In the Medal Competition only those targets that actually count for medals are to be witnessed, certified and forwarded to the secretary-treasurer for verification and record.

In order that the conditions may be uniform and eliminate as much as possible the special conditions in regard to wind, etc., that may exist at the different places where the matches may be held, the shooters should be protected at the firing point by a shelter. This may be either the regular shooting house of the club, or, if the shooting is done in the open, by a suitable tent or temporary frame structure having an opening in the direction of the target; the other three sides being inclosed. The building or tent should be large enough to accommodate also the officer or committee in charge of the match, so that the shooter may be at all times in sight of the officer in charge of the range at the time the score is made. A table of suitable size should be provided near the firing point for holding ammunition and for the convenience of the competitor to clean his arm in those events where cleaning is allowed. The firing point should be plainly marked and so located as to be at least two feet from any timbers, guards, ropes, tables, etc.

INSTRUCTIONS TO U. S. R. A. OFFICERS IN CHARGE OF THE CHAMPIONSHIP CONTESTS

Supplies consisting of numbered and certified targets, score cards, record blanks, a copy of the rules and regulations, etc., will be furnished by the secretary-treasurer on the requisition of the local U. S. R. A. representative. Such supplies shall be used only in the matches, and all used and unused supplies shall be returned to the secretary-treasurer at the close of the contests. The target and supply account of the club must balance.

A governor or other officer of the U. S. R. A. will be appointed in each locality where the matches are to be held to act as range officer, represent the association, and have charge of the contests. This governor or officer shall *personally measure the range to verify the distance* and see that all the conditions of the matches are strictly complied with. He will also see that at least one other person familiar with the rules is present to witness all the shooting and he shall certify to the correctness of each score and the conditions, by signing the score card when the score is completed, and all the targets of each competitor shall be signed by both witnesses.

The other duties in detail of the governor or officer in charge of the matches are as follows: When a competitor expresses his intention of entering a match, a score card is made out in his name and delivered to him on the payment of the higher entrance fee (unless the competitor exhibits a membership card bearing the date of the current year, in which case he is entitled to the lower entrance fee). These score cards are to be issued in numerical order, and when more than one contestant wishes to shoot at the same time, the man holding the score card first issued is entitled to the preference of position and time. When the contestant is ready to shoot, he hands his score card to the governor or other officer of the association, who thereupon issues the required targets numbered consecutively, with the name of the competitor and the number of his score card written on each target for identification.

The arm of the competitor is then inspected to make sure that it complies with the rules and regulations. The sights must be carefully inspected and the trigger-pull tested by weighing in *just before the score is begun.*

The records for which blanks are provided on the score card with reference to the arm, ammunition, etc., must all be filled in. The competitor's first target may then be placed in position. As soon as the contestant begins his score, the time is taken from the firing of the first shot in Matches A and B and in the Corresponding Indoor Championships, and the entire score must be completed within one hour from this time. Scores in Match G must be completed within 30 minutes after firing the first shot.

In Matches C, D, E, and F the time is taken from the command "Fire," and the five shots must be fired within the specified time limit in each case and a record is made of the actual elapsed time of each string which must be written on the corresponding targets later when they are brought to the firing point. The announcing of intermediate times or seconds is not allowed.

Ten shots are to be fired at each target in Matches A and B, and five shots at each target in Matches C, D, E, F, and G, and in all the Indoor Matches. After the score is completed, the separate targets are scored in regular order as shot and the value of the shots as filled in the score card are checked from the targets, *making corrections from the targets, if mistakes have been made by the markers.* After filling in and signing the score cards, the duplicate is handed to the competitor and the original preserved for record.

The targets are then signed by the governor and preserved until the expiration of the period during which the matches are held, when all targets, original score cards, and all other supplies, used and unused, are to be sent to the United States Revolver Association, addressed to the secretary-treasurer.

It is recommended that all scores after being shot, verified, etc., be wrapped in paper in separate packages, marked with the competitor's name, and that no one be permitted to handle and examine these targets after they have been scored and certified to.

The U. S. R. A. League

The League is an alliance or compact between the clubs participating, the details and conditions of which vary slightly from year to year, being embodied in a signed contract.

Any locality having six or more paid-up members in the Association may apply for the appointment of an official U. S. R. A. representative and by accepting the conditions and signing the contract, enter a team.

U. S. R. A. League Agreement for 1914–15.

Entrance Fees.—Each club with paid-up affiliation in the U. S. R.

A. shall pay an entrance fee of $10, others $15; this to cover cost of prizes only.

Expense.—The association shall furnish all targets to the clubs and shall pay the transportation from the association to the clubs and pay for all necessary telegrams to or from the secretary-treasurer, and an accurate account of these charges to be kept by the secretary and the amount to be charged back to the clubs, each club paying an equal amount. This is not to exceed $10.

Secretaries of the clubs where shooting nights and distance will permit are to use the mail, others the telegraph in the cheapest form. Results of the week MUST reach the secretary by noon of the next Monday after the shoot. The press has no use for stale news. Clubs shall pay a fine of $1 for each failure to report on time; the fines to go into the club fund for expenses.

Targets are to be sent to the various clubs prepaid. Only clubs which guarantee to stay through the series will be allowed to enter.

Shooting Night.—Clubs may shoot on one or two evenings of the week most convenient for them, but it must be the same evenings each week all through the match, unless a change be authorized by the secretary-treasurer. Any club may be allowed at the discretion of the executive committee to divide their shooters into two divisions and have two shooting nights a week. The membership of the divisions must be kept distinct, that is, a man may not change from one division to another and each division must have its regular shooting night. Matches not shot according to the above may be forfeited.

Teams to consist of five men, but each club may at its option shoot in any match from five to ten men and pick the scores of the highest five. *Qualifications, paid-up membership in the U. S. R. A.* and good standing in the local club. *A man may shoot on the team of but one club.* The scores of members in arrears for dues may be forfeited.

Conditions.—Revolvers and pistols will be allowed on equal terms, but both must comply with the U. S. R. A. rules. Five strings of five shots each will be required for each man. Target, Standard American. Distance, twenty yards. Each individual score to be completed within twenty-five minutes from the time of firing the first shot.

Scoring.—Official scoring to be done by the secretary-treasurer. In close matches, where the count of doubtful shots will determine the winner, at least two of the members of the executive committee shall be called upon to assist the secretary in scoring these shots.

Supervision.—Members of the executive committee and U. S. R. A. governors shall supervise matches within their jurisdiction, and certify that all U. S. R. A. conditions have been fulfilled. *Any score not so certified may be protested,* by any competitor and at the discretion of a majority of the executive committee may be thrown out.

Individual and club ties to be shot off.

Protests from the decision of any U. S. R. A. official may be made in writing to the secretary-treasurer, if mailed within 48 hours after the decision has been brought to the attention of the person or persons feeling aggrieved. Each person concerned in making the protest must forward $1, which will be returned if the protest is sustained, otherwise forfeited to the association treasury.

In General.—The series to begin as quickly as arrangements can be made. Matches to be shot weekly.

Targets will be furnished marked for identification, and must be used only for the match assigned and for no other purpose. For obvious reasons match targets must be jealously guarded and their individual identity carefully preserved. Clubs may purchase from the U. S. R. A. similar targets for practice purposes.

Scores on mixed targets may be forfeited.

Clubs will be classified in groups of four matches to begin the week of ....

Entries to close ....

Fraud.—Any person found guilty by the executive committee of the U. S. R. A. of cheating, evading or attempting to evade the regulations governing these contests, shall be debarred from all U. S. R. A. contests until reinstated by a vote of the members at an annual meeting of this association.

We hereby agree to all the above conditions and make application to enter a team in the U. S. R. A. League. Our preferred shooting day of the week is ....

Signed: ....

Date: ....

Witnesses:

RECORDS

The following records have been made under the United States Revolver Association rules since their adoption:

50 *Shots:*

    April 26, 1903—J. E. Gorman, San Francisco, Cal.   458
    Sept. 7, 1904—Dr. I. R. Calkins, Springfield, Mass.   465
    June 6, 1911—J. E. Gorman, San Francisco, Cal..   467
    Nov. 26, 1911—John A. Dietz, New York, N. Y.

8	8	9	9	10	10	10	10	10	10—94
9	9	9	9	10	10	10	10	10	10—96
8	8	9	9	10	10	10	10	10	10—94
9	9	9	9	9	10	10	10	10	10—95
8	9	9	10	10	10	10	10	10	10—96

    — 475

30 *Shots:*

    April 26, 1903—J. E. Gorman, San Francisco, Cal.   273
    Sept. 7, 1904—Dr. I. R. Calkins, Springfield Mass.   284
    Nov. 26, 1911—John A. Dietz, New York, N. Y.   284

20 *Shots:*

    April 26, 1903—J. E. Gorman, San Francisco, Cal.   185
    Sept. 7, 1904—Dr. I. R. Calkins, Springfield, Mass.   188
    Nov. 26, 1911—John A. Dietz, New York, N. Y...   190
    Oct. 3, 1913—A. P. Lane, New York, N. Y......   191

10 *Shots:*

    April 26, 1903—J. E. Gorman, San Francisco, Cal.   94
    Oct. 3, 1913—A. P. Lane, New York, N. Y......   96

50 *Shots:*

    March, 1902—W. E. Petty, New York, N. Y.....   439
    June 11, 1903—Dr. W. H. Luckett, New York,
      N. Y.   464
    March 4, 1904—S. E. Sears, St. Louis, Mo.
                95 96 96 95 96—   478

30 *Shots:*

    March, 1902—W. E. Petty, New York, N. Y.....   271
    June 11, 1903—Dr. W. H. Luckett, New York,
      N. Y.   275
    March 4, 1904—S. E. Sears, St. Louis, Mo......   287

20 *Shots:*

    March, 1902—W. E. Petty, New York, N. Y....   177
    March, 1903—Dr. W. H. Luckett, New York,
      N. Y.   178

June 11, 1903—Dr. W. H. Luckett, New York,
  N. Y. 184
March 4, 1904—S. E. Sears, St. Louis, Mo...... 191

10 *Shots:*
March, 1903—Dr. W. H. Luckett, New York,
  N. Y. 93
March 4, 1904—S. E. Sears, St. Louis, Mo...... 96
June 11, 1904—J. B. Crabtree, Springfield, Mass. 98
Nov. 15, 1907—C. C. Crossman, St. Louis, Mo... 100

MILITARY REVOLVER, RAPID FIRE, 50 YARDS

75 *Shots;* in strings of 5 shots in 15 seconds:
Sept., 1902—Lieut. R. H. Sayre, Sea Girt, N. J... 579
Sept. 16, 1904—Thomas Anderton, Creedmoor,
  N. Y. 585
Sept., 1910—Col. W. H. Whigam, Chicago, Ill.... 59ʸ
Sept., 1911—A. P. Lane, Sea Girt, N. J.......... 605
Sept., 1912—Dr. J. H. Snook, Columbus, O....... 621
Sept., 1913—Dr. J. H. Snook, Columbus, O....... 625
Sept., 1914—C. M. McCutcheon, Denver, Col.

$$
\begin{array}{ccccc}
9 & 9 & 8 & 8 & 7-41 \\
10 & 9 & 9 & 9 & 8-45 \\
10 & 10 & 8 & 8 & 7-43 \\
10 & 10 & 9 & 8 & 8-45 \\
9 & 9 & 9 & 8 & 6-41 \\
\end{array}
$$

— 215

$$
\begin{array}{ccccc}
9 & 9 & 9 & 8 & 8-34 * \\
9 & 8 & 8 & 8 & 7-40 \\
10 & 10 & 9 & 8 & 7-44 \\
10 & 9 & 8 & 8 & 7-42 \\
10 & 10 & 9 & 9 & 8-46 \\
\end{array}
$$

— 206

$$
\begin{array}{ccccc}
10 & 9 & 8 & 8 & 6-41 \\
10 & 9 & 8 & 9 & 6-42 \\
10 & 9 & 8 & 6 & 6-39 \\
10 & 10 & 9 & 8 & 7-44 \\
9 & 9 & 8 & 8 & 6-40 \\
\end{array}
$$

— 206

Grand Total 627

* Penalized best shot in this string for over time.

141

25 *Shots;* in strings of 5 shots in 15 seconds:
Sept., 1902—Thomas Anderton, Sea Girt, N. J.. 206
Sept., 1910—Samuel Peterson 215
Sept., 1913—C. M. McCutchen, Denver Col.... 217

Sept., 1914—Dr. J. H. Snook, Columbus, O.

10	10	9	8	8	45
10	10	10	9	7	46
10	9	9	8	7	43
10	9	9	9	7	44
10	9	9	8	7	43

— 221

POCKET REVOLVER, 50 YARDS

25 *Shots*; in strings of 5 shots in 30 seconds.
Sept. 1909—C. W. Klett, San Francisco, Cal.... 203
Sept. 1911—A. P. Lane, New York, N. Y. 211
Sept. 1914—Dr. J. H. Snook, Columbus, O.

10	10	9	8	6	43
10	10	9	9	7	45
10	9	7	7	5	38
10	9	9	8	8	44
10	10	9	8	7	44

— 214

20 YARDS (INDOORS)

March, 1909—W. G. Kreig, Chicago, Ill. 190
March, 1921—Dr. M. R. Morse, St. Louis, Mo... 202
March, 1912—John A. Dietz, New York, N. Y. .. 205
March, 1913—Hans Roedder, New York, N. Y... 206
March, 1914—Dr. J. H. Snook, Columbus, O. 213

PISTOL, 50 YARDS

50 *Shots:*
April 4, 1903—Thomas Anderton, Walnut Hill,
Mass.

10	10	10	9	10	10	10	10	10	10—99
9	9	10	10	10	9	10	9	9	9—94
9	10	10	9	9	9	10	10	10	10—96
10	10	10	10	10	10	10	10	10	9—99
8	9	9	8	10	9	10	10	9	10—92

— 480

30 *Shots:*
  March 21, 1903—E. E. Patridge, Walnut Hill,
    Mass. 287
  April 4, 1903—Thomas Anderton, Walnut Hill,
    Mass. 289
  Feb. 1, 1914—F. J. Dreher, Denver, Col.......... 291

20 *Shots:*
  March 21, 1903—E. E. Patridge, Walnut Hill,
    Mass. 192
  April 4, 1903—Thomas Anderton, Walnut Hill,
    Mass. 193
  Feb. 1, 1914—F. J. Dreher, Denver, Col.......... 196

10 *Shots:*
  March 21, 1903—E. E. Patridge, Walnut Hill,
    Mass. 96
  April 4, 1903—Thomas Anderton, Walnut Hill,
    Mass. 99
  Feb. 1, 1914—F. J. Dreher, Denver, Col.......... 100

PISTOL, 20 YARDS

50 *Shots:*
  March 2, 1902—Lieut. R. H. Sayre, New York,
    N. Y. 448
  March, 1903—Thomas Anderton, Boston, Mass... 460
  March 25, 1908—L. R. Hatch, Portland, Me...... 462
  Dec. 1, 1909—J. E. Gorman, San Francisco, Cal.. 471
  March, 1911—George Armstrong, Seattle, Wash.. 473
  Jan. 25, 1912—George Armstrong, Portland, Ore.. 478
  March 4, 1912—George Armstrong, Portland, Ore.

                10 9 10 10 10 10 10 10 10 10—99
                10 10 10 9 10 9 10 9 10 10—97
                10 10 10 10 9 9 10 10 8 10—96
                10 10 10 9 10 10 9 10 10 9—97
                 9 9 10 9 10 8 9 10 10 8—92
                                              ——
                                              481

30 *Shots:*
  March, 1902—Lieut. R. H. Sayre, New York, N.Y. 260
  March, 1903—Thomas Anderton, Boston, Mass... 276
  March 20, 1908—Lieut. R. H. Sayre, New York,
    N. Y. 278
  March 25, 1908—L. R. Hatch, Portland, Me...... 279

Dec. 1, 1909—J. E. Gorman, San Francisco, Cal.. 283
March, 1911—George Armstrong, Seattle, Wash.. 284
Jan. 11, 1912—George Armstrong, Portland, Ore.. 287
March 4, 1912—George Armstrong, Portland, Ore. 292

20 *Shots:*
March, 1902—Lieut. R. H. Sayre, New York, N.Y. 173
March, 1903—Thomas Anderton, Boston, Mass... 189
Dec. 1, 1909—J. E. Gorman, San Francisco, Cal... 192
Jan. 11, 1912—George Armstrong, Portland, Ore.. 193
March 4, 1912—George Armstrong, Portland, Ore. 196

10 *Shots:*
March, 1903—Thomas Anderton, Boston, Mass... 92
March 24, 1906—John A. Dietz, New York, N.Y. 93
March 24, 1906—J. B. Crabtree. Springfield, Mass. 95
May 18, 1908—F. L. Hayden, Portland, Me....... 97
May 20, 1910—A. M. Poindexter, Red Bank, N.J. 100
April 16, 1914—Dr. D. Atkinson, West View, Pa. 100

Appendix 2

This match is an annual contest, authorized by the National Board for the Promotion of Rifle Practice and is conducted under the auspices of the National Rifle Association of America. In alternate years the match is held at a National shooting tournament, at a State or Federal range having sufficient facilities. These National shooting tournaments have been held at Camp Perry, Ohio, and Sea Girt, New Jersey. At these tournaments, in addition to the National Pistol Matches, there are a number of other pistol and revolver matches with extensive prize lists.

Every other year the National Pistol Match is conducted in connection with the National Divisional Matches, which in 1914 were held at Sea Girt, New Jersey; Jacksonville, Florida; Sparta, Wisconsin; Fort Reily, Kansas; and Portland, Oregon.

The following are the conditions of this match:

(a) Open to the Army, Navy, Marine Corps, cadets United States Military Academy, midshipmen United States Naval Academy, the Organized Militia, the Naval Militia, members of the National Rifle Association of America and affiliated clubs, members of the United States Revolver Association, universities, colleges, and military schools and colleges.

(b) Distances and classes of fire:

Slow Fire (30 Seconds per Shot)

	Yards
2 scores (7 shots each)	50
2 scores (7 shots each)	75

Rapid Fire, (30 Seconds per Score)

	Yards
2 scores (7 shots each)	25
2 scores (7 shots each)	50

Rapid Fire (15 Seconds per Score)

2 scores (7 shots each)	15
2 scores (7 shots each)	25

(c) Targets: Target L will be used for all firing.

(d) Position: Without body or artificial rest; one hand only to be used.

(e) Arm: Colt's automatic pistol, calibre .45, government model; trigger-pull not less than six pounds.

(f) Ammunition: The Ordnance Department shall manufacture and issue ammunition for use in preliminary practice and in the National divisional pistol matches; all such ammunition to be as nearly as practicable of the same date of manufacture and of the same quality.

(g) Sights: No alteration of sights will be allowed. The front or rear sights may be blackened according to the judgment of the competitor.

(h) Cleaning: Pieces can be cleaned upon the completion of the score. In competitions at more than one distance, cleaning will be permitted between distances. While such cleaning will be permitted, it will not be required.

(i) Procedure, Rapid Fire; Pistol: The officer in charge of the line will command "Load." The magazine will be inserted in the pistol, the pistol loaded with one cartridge therefrom, and the safety lock engaged with the thumb of the right hand. When all is ready in the pit, the targets to be fired will be drawn fully down (the rear targets being blank or targets of another class than those being fired upon) and a red flag hoisted at the centre target. When the red flag is displayed, the officer in charge of the firing line will command "Ready," when the safety lock will be disengaged and the position of "Raise pistol" assumed.

The firing line being ready, the pit is signalled or telephoned "Ready on the firing line." When this signal is received in the pit, the red flag is waved and lowered, and five seconds thereafter the targets appear. At exactly the proper number of seconds after the target is in position the range officer commands or signals "Down," having preceded this command two or three seconds by the warning command or signal "Ready." The target must be fully exposed and stationary for the number of seconds called for in the match and then must be withdrawn as quickly as possible. The number and value of the hits and the number of misses will be signalled in the usual manner after the score has been fired.

In case of a defective cartridge or a disabled pistol, or when more than seven hits are made on the target, the score will be repeated. In case a competitor fires on the wrong target only such shots as he may have fired on his own target will be counted on his score. He will be given misses for the remainder of his score.

Rules: As laid down in the *Small Arms Firing Manual, 1913*, except as herein modified.

Prizes: One gold medal to the competitor making the highest aggregate score, one silver medal to the competitor making the second highest score, and one bronze medal to the competitor making the third highest score in each National divisional competition. To be eligible to win a prize in any National divisional pistol match, a competitor must be a resident or a member of an organization located within the division in which the competition occurs. No competitor shall be eligible to win prizes in more than one National divisional competition.

Appendix 3

Target Practice Regulations adopted by the

War Department

(*In Effect After Jan. 1st, 1914*)

The following is a digest of the target practice prescribed for the U. S. Army, using the regulation Colt automatic pistol, calibre .45, with service ammunition, as given in the *Small Arms Firing Manual* (War Department Document No. 442). A very excellent and complete program for target practice is contemplated. Chapter 9 is devoted to "Preliminary Drills; Position and Aiming Drills," in which the soldier is trained in all the motions of aiming and firing, snapping the weapon. Exercises are provided for dismounted and mounted soldiers. Chapters 10, 11, and 12 prescribe the actual practice shooting with complete rules, regulations, and methods of procedure, together with illustrations and diagrams.

The regulation target practice is divided into two courses: the dismounted course and the mounted course, each of which is separate and complete in itself. The following schedule shows the general target practice scheme of each course, a score in all cases consisting of five consecutive shots.

Target Practice Schedule
Dismounted Course

	NO. OF SHOTS
Instruction Practice:	
Slow fire, at 15 and 25 yards, minimum of 1 score at each range. Target L. Time limit, none.....	10
Rapid fire, at 15 and 25 yards, minimum of 2 scores at each range. Target L. Time, 20 seconds per score	20
Quick fire, at 15 and 25 yards, minimum of 2 scores at each range. Target E—Bobbing. Time, 3 seconds per shot at 15 yards; 4 seconds per shot	

at 25 yards...................................... 20

Record Practice:
   Rapid fire, at 25 yards, 2 scores. Target L. Time,
      20 seconds for each score...................... 10
   Quick fire, at 15 and 25 yards, 2 scores at each
      range. Target E—Bobbing. Time, 3 seconds per
      shot at 15 yards; 4 seconds per shot at 25 yards. 20

Expert Test:
   Rapid fire, at 50 yards, 1 score. Target L. Time,
      30 seconds per score.......................... 5
   Quick fire, at 15 and 25 yards, 1 score at each
      range. Target E—Bobbing. Time, 3 seconds
      per shot at 15 yards; 4 seconds per shot at 25
      yards 10
                                                      ——
         Total 95

MOUNTED COURSE

Instruction Practice:
   Dismounted—
   Slow fire, 15 yards, minimum of 2 scores. Target
      L. Time limit, none........................... 10
   Quick fire, 15 yards, minimum of 2 scores. Target
      M—Bobbing. Time, 3 seconds per shot........ 10
   Mounted—
   Halt; minimum of 2 scores; one to the right and
      one to the left. Target M—Bobbing. Range,
      10 yards. Time, 3 seconds per shot............ 10
   Walk; minimum of 2 scores; one score firing to
      the right while moving to the left and one score
      firing to the left while moving to the right around
      the circumference of circle about 12 ft. in diam-
      eter tangent to the track at the firing point. Tar-
      get M—Bobbing. Range, 10 yards. Time, 3
      seconds per shot.............................. 10
   Gallop; minimum of 8 scores. Target M. Range,
      10 yards. Time governed by gait of at least 12
      miles an hour................................. 40
         [*Note:*—Five M targets are placed 10 yards
      from the track and 10 yards apart (20 yards
      apart for the revolver). Each trooper makes
      eight circlings of the track (four in each direc-
      tion) firing four scores to the right and four
      to the left.]

149

Record Practice:

Halt; quick fire. Target M—Bobbing. 2 scores
1 to the right, 1 to the left. Range, 10 yards.
Time, 3 seconds per shot...................... 10

Gallop; Target M. Range, 10 and 14 yards. 4
scores—2, firing to the right while circling to the
left; 2, firing to the left while circling to the
right 20

Time governed by gait of at least 12 miles
an hour.

[*Note:*—Three of the five M targets (the
first, the center, and the last targets) of the gallop stage, Instruction Practice, are set at an angle
of 45 degrees to the track, and the trooper in
making the run fires at each of these when facing
them at about 14 yards range. The firing of the
full score and the direction of the shots is therefore as follows: Right front, right, right front,
right, and right rear. In making the left hand
run, two targets are set at an angle and the
firing is in the following order: Left, left front,
left, left front, left.]

Expert Test:

Halt; 1 score. Five E targets—Bobbing; unknown
angles. Range, 8½ to 15 yards. Time, 2 seconds
per shot 5

Gallop; 1 score; group of three M targets. Range,
10 and 14 yards; 3 shots to right advancing and
2 shots to left returning. Time governed by gait
of at least 12 miles per hour.................. 5

[*Note:*—Two of the targets are set at an
angle as in the gallop stage, Record Practice,
the firing being right front, right, right rear, in
advancing; and left front, left, in returning.]

Gallop, extended; 2 scores. Range, 5 to 15 yards.
Time governed by gait......................... 10

[*Note:*—Targets arranged as follows: Target F 5 yards to the right; 20 yards further along
track, Target E, 7 yards to the right; 30 yards
further, Target M, 10 yards to the left; 20 yards
further, Target M, 10 yards to the left; 30 yards
further, Target M, 15 yards to the right. Two
runs are made firing at the targets in the order
named.]

Total number of shots........................ 130

Explanatory Notes, etc.

Timing: —Intervals of time are measured from the last note of the signal or command, "Commence firing," to the last note or word of "Cease firing."

Targets:—Target L is illustrated in Figure 79. Targets E, F, and M are full size silhouette figures of men in the kneeling, prone and standing positions, respectively. When "bobbing" target is prescribed, it refers to an operating device for turning the targets 90 degrees on a vertical axis by means of ropes. The target is thus made to turn so as to appear edgewise and flatwise from the firing point and remains flatwise or "exposed" for the number of seconds stated in the time limit for each shot, and "turned from view" between shots for an interval of 3 to 5 seconds.

Procedure:—In quick fire the soldier stands at the firing point, pistol loaded with 5 cartridges, hammer down (in mounted practice hammer cocked at safe), weapon in holster, flap, if any, buttoned. Upon the first exposure of the target the soldier draws and fires, or attempts to fire, one shot at the target before it is turned from view and keeps the weapon in hand until he has fired five shots at successive exposures of the target to complete the score.

Qualification Scores: Dismounted Course—Sixty *per cent.* of the aggregate possible score of the Instruction Practice for advancement to Record Practice and 80 *per cent.* of the latter for advancement to Expert Test. In Expert Test, 50 out of a possible 60. *Mounted Course*—Fifty *per cent.* of the aggregate possible score of the Instruction Practice for advancement to Record Practice and 70 *per cent.* of the latter for advancement to Expert Test. In Expert Test, 13 out of a possible 20.

Competitions:—In every alternate year department pistol competitions are held simultaneously with the department rifle competitions at places designated by the department commanders.

Organized Militia Target Practice

The prescribed course in effect in 1914 is adapted to the service revolvers. Five shots constitute a score. All shooting is on Target L. The course is divided into Instruction Practice and Record Practice.

Instruction Practice:

Slow Fire: Range 15, 25, and 50 yards; one score at each range. Time limit, none.

Rapid Fire: Range 15, 25, and 50 yards; two scores at each range.

Time limit, 30 seconds per score.

Rapid Fire: Range 15 and 25 yards; two scores at each range. Time limit, 15 seconds per score.

Record Practice:

Rapid Fire: Range 25 and 50 yards; two scores at each range. Time limit, 30 seconds per score.

Rapid Fire: Range 15 and 25 yards; two scores at each range. Time limit, 15 seconds per score.

The rules, regulations, and procedure are the same as those governing the U. S. Army practice.

Qualification scores are as follows out of a possible 400: Second classman, 250; first classman, 300, and expert pistol shot, 320. Insignia badges and pins are awarded to those qualifying.

U. S. Navy Target Practice Regulations

The new firing regulations and prescribed course of practice with the automatic pistol are as follows:[1]

Each officer or man may fire the pistol course for credits once per year while attached to each division.

The firing in the pistol course may be done at any range.

Any target may be used.

The course is as follows:

Position	Slow Fire	Rapid fire
Prone	5 shots	1 string of 5 shots
Kneeling	5 shots	1 string of 5 shots
Squatting	5 shots	1 string of 5 shots
Standing	5 shots	1 string of 5 shots
Total number of shots 20		20
Aggregate number of shots		40
Possible aggregate score		200

All men are eligible to compete for prizes in this course once per year while attached to each division.

The value of a prize in the pistol course is $1.

When scoring in the pistol courses, in order to prevent the markers from knowing the names of the individuals who are firing, the name of the firer will not be announced by the scorer, but the number of the target he fires upon will be substituted for his name.

Before automatic pistols are brought to a range, the magazines

---

1. Reproduced from *Small Arms Firing Regulation U. S. Navy, 1917.*

should be removed and kept removed at all times except while the pistol is in actual use at the firing point.

Under no circumstances should any one handle a pistol, loaded or unloaded, except when he is on the firing line fully abreast of the firers, and the pistol should never be pointed in any other direction than the front.

NOTES ON PISTOL PRACTICE

When a pistol is first taken in hand it should be examined to make sure that it is not loaded.

Both the front sight and the rear sighting groove should be blackened. When the pistol is aimed the front sight should be seen through the middle of the rear sighting groove and the top of the front sight should be flush with the top of the groove. The part of the target to be aimed at must be determined by practice. With most pistols at 25 yards the aim is usually taken at the bottom edge or in the bottom part of the bullseye, and at 50 yards in the centre or in the upper part of the bullseye.

Grasp the stock of the pistol as high up as you can so that the barrel, hand, and arm are as nearly as possible in one straight line. The thumb should be extended along the upper part of the frame. The second joint of the forefinger should be on the trigger.

Start with a light grip and gradually squeeze with the whole hand, the trigger finger squeezing gradually back as the grip is tightened, and continue squeezing without a jerk until the pistol fires. Decide to call the hold and to keep the right eye open.

If the hits are bunched to one side they can be moved to the right by increasing the pressure of the thumb against the left side of the pistol or to the left by decreasing the pressure.

Snapping—that is, aiming and squeezing the trigger with the pistol not loaded—is most valuable practice. No man should load and fire until he has snapped several times to get acquainted with the trigger pull of the pistol. Expert pistol shots do a great deal of snapping instead of a great deal of firing. Steady holding can be acquired only by much snapping practice.

In the prone position the right elbow has excellent support on the ground. In the kneeling position the firer may kneel on either knee. Kneeling on the left knee affords an excellent rest on the right knee for the elbow. In the squatting position both elbows rest on the knees. In the standing position face the target squarely, or nearly so. Stand upright, not craning the head forward, and extend the arm to its full stretch.

A coach should be at each firing point. In addition to the general duties of a coach, his specific duties in pistol practice are: (1) to stand slightly behind the right side of the firer in order to prevent the pistol being pointed away from the front, (2) to see that the pistol is not loaded until the proper time, (3) to require the firer to explain the line of sight, (4) to see that the firer takes the proper position and holds the pistol properly, (5) to require the firer to snap several times and to call the hold, (6) to see that the firer loads properly, and (7) to see that the pistol is unloaded before it leaves the firer's hands.

Appendix 4

The board of officers appointed by the Secretary of War (Special Order No. 305, Dec. 28, 1906) to test automatic pistols and revolvers met at the Springfield Armory, Springfield, Mass., on January 15, 1907. The board consisted of: Col. Philip Reade, 23rd Infantry; Maj. Joseph T. Dickman, 13th Cavalry; Capt. Guy H. Preston, 13th Cavalry; Capt. Ernest D. Scott, Artillery Corps, and Capt. John H. Rice, Ordnance Department.

The weapons referred to the board by the Chief of Ordnance for examination and test with their weights (unloaded) were as follows:

Automatic Pistols, Calibre .45	Lbs.	Oz.
The Colt	2	2½
The Luger	2	8
The Savage	2	3
The Knoble (single action)	2	11½
The Knoble (double action)	2	10½
The Bergmann	2	3½
The White Merrill	2	6½
Double Action Revolvers, Calibre .45		
The Colt	2	7
The Smith & Wesson	2	6
Automatic Revolver, calibre .45		
The Webley-Fosbury	1	10

Programme of tests of Automatic Pistols[1]

1. Examination of pistol as to design, appearance, balance, suitability for mounted troops, etc.

2. Special examination as to safety features.

3. Dismounting and assembling. The times required for each of the

---

1. The tests for revolvers were similar, with suitable slight modifications.

following operations:

(a) To dismount the breech and magazine mechanism, with the exception of the magazine catch.

(b) To complete dismounting.

(c) To assemble, except the breech and magazine mechanism.

(d) To complete assembling.

4. The number of—

(a) Pins and screws.

(b) Small springs.

(c) Other parts.

5. The number and kind of tools required to dismount and assemble.

6. Twenty rounds to be fired to observe working of pistol. The above tests will be made with the pistol in the hands of and operated by the inventor or his representative, if present.

7. Velocity at 25 feet, mean of 5 shots.

8. Accuracy and penetration at 75 feet; 10 shots for accuracy, 5 for penetration.

9. Rapidity with accuracy; target 6 by 2 feet, range 100 feet. Number of shots fired to be three times the capacity of clip. Pistol fired from hand. Time and number of hits to be noted in each case. To be conducted by representative of company, if present. Firing to begin with chamber and magazine empty, and clips or holders arranged as desired by firer.

10. Rapidity at will. Same as preceding test, except that the pistol will be fired without aim into a butt at short range, and hits will not be considered.

11. Endurance. Pistol will then be fired deliberately 500 rounds as a self-loader, cooling after each 50 rounds.

12. Velocity. Same as paragraph 7, above.

13. Decreased charges. Pistol to be fired 12 rounds as a self-loader with cartridge in which the powder charge has been decreased so that the first four will give pressure of 25 *per cent.* less, the second four 15 per cent. less, and the last four 10 *per cent.* less than the service pressure.

14. Excessive charges. Pistol to be fired 5 times as a single loader,

with cartridges in which the charge of powder is increased to produce a pressure in the chamber 25 *per cent.* greater than the regular pressure.

15. Pierced primers. Pistol will be fired once with a cartridge in which the primer has been thinned so as to insure piercing. Two rounds will then be fired to observe action.

16. Dust. With the mechanism closed and both ends of the barrel tightly corked pistol will be exposed, in a box prepared for that purpose, to a blast of fine sand for one minute. The surplus sand may then be removed by blowing thereon, jarring the piece, or wiping with the bare hand only.

The Magazine should be—

(a) Empty when exposed to dust.

(b) Loaded when exposed to dust.

In both cases pistol should be used as a self-loader, and in the second the cartridge may be removed and wiped, then reloaded. In case of self-loading failures to work in either case the piece will be tried by operating by hand.

17. Rust. The mechanism will be thoroughly cleansed of grease by boiling in a solution of soda, the ends of the barrel tightly corked and the pistol then placed in a saturated solution of sal-ammoniac for five minutes. After being hung up indoors for 22 hours, five shots will be fired into a sand butt, using pistol as a self-loader. In case the self-loading mechanism fails to work, the pistol will then be tried by operating by hand.

18. Supplementary Tests. Any piece which successfully passes the foregoing tests may be subjected to such supplementary tests, or repetitions of previous ones, to further determine its endurance or other qualities as may be prescribed by the Chief of Ordnance or by the board.

General Remarks. During the above tests the pistol will be entirely in the hands of the board, except when specifically stated otherwise, and no alterations or repairs other than those possible on the ground will be allowed, except by special permission of the board. If the pistol fails in any test the remainder of the programme may be discontinued in the discretion of the board.

In case of misfires the cartridges will be opened to determine cause, and if due to the ammunition the test will be repeated.

The board thoroughly tested the merits of the various arms submitted to them, and reported in 1907 the conclusion that in principle the automatic pistol was better suited for service use than the revolver.

The board also recommended a .45-calibre pistol. At the same time it was stated that the automatic pistol had not been sufficiently developed in reliability to warrant its adoption. A service test was ordered, and the Colt's Patent Firearms Manufacturing Company and the Savage Arms Company submitted automatic pistols according to specifications.

Two troops of cavalry were assigned to make this test and the report showed that neither pistol had reached a desired proficiency. The matter was then turned over to the Ordnance Department for further experiment. Both of the arms companies were given time to improve their pistols under the direction of Brig.-Gen. William Crozier, Chief of Ordnance; Lieut.-Col. John T. Thompson, Ordnance Department, and Capt. Gilbert H. Stewart, Ordnance Department. After a number of informal tests by these officers, which demonstrated that the arms companies had approached the standard set by the Ordnance Department, a new board of officers was appointed to determine which of the two pistols should be adopted. This board consisted of Majors Kenneth Morton and Walter G. Penfield and Lieutenants C. A. Meals and Arthur D. Minick, Ordnance Department.

Two pistols were submitted to the board, one by the Savage Arms Company, the other by the Colt's Patent Firearms Manufacturing Company, and the tests were conducted in March, 1911. The ammunition used was of recent manufacture by the Union Metallic Cartridge Company, had a jacketed 230-grain bullet, and was loaded to give a muzzle velocity of 800 f.s. The weight of the Savage was found to be 2 lbs. 8 oz.; the Colt 2 lbs. 7 oz. The mechanical safety of both is convenient for operation with the thumb of the firing hand. Time required to complete dismounting, Savage 29.6 seconds, Colt 24.5 seconds.; to assemble, except the magazine, Savage 5 min. 10.5 sec., Colt 4 min. 50 sec.; to complete assembling, additional time, Savage 28.5 sec., Colt 12.5 sec. The number of parts in each pistol was then counted, and found to be as follows: Total components, Savage 40, including four in magazine; Colt 61, including seven in magazine. The number and kind of tools required to dismount and assemble the pistols were: Colt, one screwdriver; Savage, one combination tool (one screwdriver, two drifts).

Fifty rounds from each pistol were fired deliberately into a butt to observe the operation. The two pistols functioned normally. The Savage pistol ejected the empty shells upward and to the front, while the Colt ejected upward and to the right and rear. The velocity of each pistol was measured at twenty-five feet, and the mean of five shots was: Savage, 849.4 ft. per second; Colt, 828.0 ft. per second. Two targets of ten shots from each pistol were made for accuracy at seventy-five feet, using a muzzle rest, with the resulting mean radii of dispersion: Savage, first target 1.97", second target 1.97", mean 1.97"; Colt, first target .89", second target .82", mean 0.8555".

Three magazines full of cartridges were fired from each pistol at a target six feet by two feet, 100 feet distant, to test the rapidity and accuracy. The firing was begun with the chamber empty and three full magazines for each pistol with it on the table. Results:

	Savage	Colt
Time	35 sec.	28 sec.
Number of shots	24 "	21 "
Hits	22 "	21 "
Mean *radii*	7.27 "	5.85 "

The pistols were next fired for rapidity by the same persons into a butt at short range and no hits considered: Savage, 24 shots, time 16 sec.; Colt, 21 shots, time 12 sec. In all the above tests the pistols functioned normally.

The two pistols were then thoroughly examined, oiled, and fired deliberately 6,000 rounds each, being cleaned thoroughly, examined and oiled after each 1,000 rounds. Wherever examination showed the least sign of deformation it was noted. Each pistol was fired 100 rounds and then was allowed to cool while the other was fired, giving each pistol at least five minutes to cool. Firing was not begun after cooling until the hand could be placed on the slide over the barrel without discomfort. There was an interval of about two seconds between shots in the same magazine when the pistol functioned normally.

During the firing of the first 1,000, in 1h. 29m., the magazine of each pistol dropped about an inch, due to the fault of the operator. Second 1,000, in 1h. 48m., the Colt functioned perfectly; while the Savage missed fire once, jammed twice and had trouble with the bolt twice. Third 1,000, in 2h. 2m. the Colt functioned perfectly; in round 2,924 the bolt stop of the Savage broke. Fourth 1,000, in 2h. 1m., the Colt functioned perfectly; with the Savage there was a slight jam and two misfires, the bolt stop was upset. Fifth 1,000, in 2h. 6m., the Colt functioned perfectly; the Savage magazine dropped five times, the bolt stop was further upset and there were two cracks in the bolt. Sixth 1,000, the Colt again functioned perfectly, and there were five misfires with the Savage, two jams, fourteen failures of the bolt to counter re-coil fully, and a breakage of the bolt lock spring. Minute examination of the Colt pistol after this test failed to show any broken parts, the only defect being a minute bulging of the frame near the front end of the grooves and a slight upsetting of the bolt stop where it strikes the magazine follower.

The pistols were then fired five times as single loaders in a recoiling rest with cartridges in which the powder charge was increased to give a calculated chamber pressure of twenty-five *per cent*. greater than nor-mal. The Colt pistol functioned normally. The sear of the Savage broke at the fourth round. A new sear was inserted, also a new sear spring, broken in removing the broken sear. The removal of the broken sear was difficult on account of the design of the pistol, and other parts were deformed in removing the breech plug. Upon reassembling, the pistol functioned normally in the fifth round. Each pistol was fired in a recoiling rest one round, in which the primer had been thinned so as to be pierced by the firing pin. Afterward two rounds were fired auto-matically. Both pistols functioned satisfactorily. The pistols were then disassembled, cleaned, and thoroughly examined. Both were found to be in good condition, with no broken parts. All misfire cartridges were examined and no defects found.

The shock of recoil of the Savage was found much more severe than of the Colt. The experienced operators who fired several thou-sand rounds in the endurance test, in alternate five hundreds, esti-mated the fatigue of firing 500 rounds with the Savage equal to firing 2,000 rounds with the Colt.

"Of the two pistols the board is of the opinion that the Colt's is superior, because it is more reliable, the more enduring, the more eas-ily disassembled when there are broken parts to be replaced, and the more accurate. It equals in these qualities the Colt calibre .45 revolver, model 1909, while being superior to that arm in balance, safety, rapid-ity, accuracy of fire, and interchangeability. The Colt pistol embodies all the features considered essential, desirable, and preferable by the board of officers convened by S. O. 305, W. D., Washington, December 28, 1906, except that there is no automatic indicator showing that the pistol is loaded or indicator showing the number of cartridges remaining in the magazine. There are, however, a few riveted parts, and the board is uncertain whether the pistol would function properly with non-jacketed bullets. The board therefore recommends that Colt calibre .45 automatic pistol of the design submitted to the board for test be adopted for use by foot and mounted troops in the military service in consequence of its marked superiority to the present service revolvers and to any other known pistol, of its extreme reliability and endurance, and of its fulfilment of all essential requirements."

This report was approved March 23, 1911, by Col. S. E. Blunt, Ord. Dept., U. S. A., commanding Springfield Armoury, Mass.

Appendix 5

Occasionally a firearm becomes disabled by the breaking of a spring or some other part of the mechanism. All the manufacturers carry a stock of duplicate parts and any broken or worn-out part can be obtained promptly from the makers of the weapon and the replacement made with a screwdriver and a few drifts. When any of the parts become worn, the simplest and most inexpensive course to follow is to substitute new parts in the same manner.

The most frequent source of difficulty is the wearing light of the trigger-pull. This may also be corrected by the substitution of a new hammer and a new trigger; or an experienced mechanic can generally correct the difficulty with an oil stone. Inexperienced persons are liable to ruin the parts if they attempt to do this work themselves.

The barrels of the weapons after long use, especially in the open on camping expeditions, etc., become rusted or they are worn out by extensive use so as to require renewal. In such cases a new barrel may be ordered from the maker of the weapon, which should be sent to the factory to have the substitution made and the necessary fitting and finish properly executed. In the case of high-priced barrels, and especially where the barrel is part of the action, it is sometimes less expensive to have a good gunsmith bore out the interior of the barrel and insert a new sleeve instead of replacing the entire barrel.

Very often the marksman will conceive an idea or invent an improvement which will add to the convenience in manipulation or usefulness of the weapon, the reloading tools, etc. As he becomes interested in the sport he may want to try special sights, a different shape of trigger guard, matted trigger, and various other modifications and refinements, thinking they may improve his shooting.

Without the necessary mechanical skill to execute their ideas successfully all such special work should be intrusted to a competent and first-class mechanic who is equipped and prepared to execute work of this character in the best manner. The following are the names and addresses of a few of the leading manufacturers and gunsmiths, with a brief statement as to the character of work that each undertakes and specializes on:

SMITH & WESSON, SPRINGFIELD, MASS.

This company maintains a repair department, but undertakes repair, reblueing and replating only on arms of their own manufacture. A limited quantity of special work is also undertaken, provided it meets with the approval of the manufacturers as being useful, desirable, and in nowise a detriment to the weapon. All repair and special work is executed in the order in which it is received, and as a limited force is engaged in this department a delay of a week or more sometimes occurs before the work can be begun. In case of general repairs the cost of same is quoted before repairs are started.

COLT PATENT FIREARMS MANUFACTURING CO., HARTFORD, CONN.

This company maintains a repair department devoted exclusively to arms of Colt manufacture. Estimates of the cost of repairs are quoted before work is begun. Special work, reblueing and replating, is also executed in connection with Colt arms.

WINCHESTER REPEATING ARMS CO., NEW HAVEN, CONN.

Reloading tools, bullet moulds, bullets, shells, primers, etc.

UNION METALLIC CARTRIDGE CO., BRIDGEPORT, CONN.
UNITED STATES CARTRIDGE CO., LOWELL, MASS.
THE PETERS CARTRIDGE CO., CINCINNATI, OHIO.

Shells, bullets, and primers.

H. M. POPE, 18 MORRIS STREET, JERSEY CITY.

Manufacturer of the famous "Pope" barrels for rifles, revolvers, and pistols. New barrels furnished for any of the leading makes of target arms. Pope graduated automatic powder measures and reloading tools. Telescope mountings. Special work and fine repair work of all kinds.

J. E. WILBURN, 403 RIVERSIDE AVE., SPOKANE, WASH.

Specializes on very accurate and high-grade pistol and revolver barrels of .22 and .38 calibre. Fine repair work of every description.

IDEAL MANUFACTURING CO. (MARLIN FIRE ARMS CO., SUCCESSORS), NEW HAVEN, CONN.

Reloading tools, powder measures, bullet moulds, bullets, etc.

H. H. KIFFE CO., 533 BROADWAY, NEW YORK CITY.

J. P. DANNEFELSER, 19 WARREN STREET, NEW YORK CITY.

Carry a full line of smokeless powders for rifle and pistol ammunition.

(Nearly all the sporting goods dealers in the large cities carry a stock of black and smokeless powders.)

LEONAUR

ALSO FROM LEONAUR
AVAILABLE IN SOFTCOVER OR HARDCOVER WITH DUST JACKET

"AMBULANCE 464" ENCORE DES BLESSÉS *by Julien H. Bryan*—The experiences of an American Volunteer with the French Army during the First World War

THE GREAT WAR IN THE MIDDLE EAST: 1 *by W. T. Massey*—The Desert Campaigns & How Jerusalem Was Won---two classic accounts in one volume.

THE GREAT WAR IN THE MIDDLE EAST: 2 *by W. T. Massey*—Allenby's Final Triumph.

SMITH-DORRIEN *by Horace Smith-Dorrien*—Isandlwhana to the Great War.

1914 *by Sir John French*—The Early Campaigns of the Great War by the British Commander.

GRENADIER *by E. R. M. Fryer*—The Recollections of an Officer of the Grenadier Guards throughout the Great War on the Western Front.

BATTLE, CAPTURE & ESCAPE *by George Pearson*—The Experiences of a Canadian Light Infantryman During the Great War.

DIGGERS AT WAR *by R. Hugh Knyvett & G. P. Cuttriss*—"Over There" With the Australians by R. Hugh Knyvett and Over the Top With the Third Australian Division by G. P. Cuttriss. Accounts of Australians During the Great War in the Middle East, at Gallipoli and on the Western Front.

HEAVY FIGHTING BEFORE US *by George Brenton Laurie*—The Letters of an Officer of the Royal Irish Rifles on the Western Front During the Great War.

THE CAMELIERS *by Oliver Hogue*—A Classic Account of the Australians of the Imperial Camel Corps During the First World War in the Middle East.

RED DUST *by Donald Black*—A Classic Account of Australian Light Horsemen in Palestine During the First World War.

THE LEAN, BROWN MEN *by Angus Buchanan*—Experiences in East Africa During the Great War with the 25th Royal Fusiliers—the Legion of Frontiersmen.

THE NIGERIAN REGIMENT IN EAST AFRICA *by W. D. Downes*—On Campaign During the Great War 1916-1918.

THE AUXILIA OF THE ROMAN IMPERIAL ARMY *by G.L.Cheeseman*

THE MILITARY SYSTEM OF THE ROMANS *by Albert Harkness*

www.ingramcontent.com/pod-product-compliance
Lightning Source LLC
Chambersburg PA
CBHW021109090426
42738CB00006B/562